LIVING FROM THE HEART

LIVING FROM THE HEART

Healing ourselves so we can heal the world

ERIN EASTON

New Leaf Mindfulness Coaching

Reading Suggestions

This book is meant to be read slowly so that you can fully understand and experience its teachings. It is best to use the guided meditation videos to accompany the book's content. These can be found on my website, www.newleafmindfulness.com/meditation-catalog. I would suggest reading one topic per week, performing the corresponding guided meditations daily, and journaling on the questions within the meditations before you move on to the next. You will get more out of the process if you share it with others by practicing and discussing the teachings together. After completing the process, you may want to return over and over to the topics that are most challenging for you, making the practice a lifestyle rather than a one-time study.

Contents

Reading Suggestions   v
Introduction   ix

PART 1
COMING BACK HOME

1. Open to Change   3

PART 2
HEALING OURSELVES WITH KINDNESS

2. Mindful of the Body   16
3. Mindful of the Mind   42
4. Mindful of Our Emotions   65
5. Mindful of Our Spirit   89

PART 3
BUILDING A FOUNDATION OF PEACE

6. Mindfulness as a Lifestyle   110

7	The Power of Perspective	115
8	Forgiving Self and Others	125
9	Mindful Consumption	157

PART 4
REACHING OUT IN LOVE

10	Continued Self-Love	196
11	Mindful Communication	202
12	Mindfully Loving Others	234
13	Living From the Heart	268

Acknowledgments	277
About the Author	279
Resources	281

Introduction

Outside, the winds of change are screaming through the world, setting our economic, health, education, and social systems into a frenzy of uncertainty. Inside, there is stillness, a peace grounded in the true source of happiness that resides within our own heart. This peace is found through a journey of healing that begins with the intention to know ourselves, a longing to come back home and understand our inner thoughts, emotions, and aspirations and the effect they have on our presence in the world. As we observe the inner workings of self, we begin to notice that all of life is a construct of our own awareness and attention; by guiding our own mind, we can alter the world. With the hope of healing, one begins to listen to the suffering within the body and mind, accept its presence and learn from it. Within acceptance, we find peace within ourselves that develops into a peace with the external world. It is within this peaceful state that we reconnect with our heart center, or our true essence, which is founded in **love, peace, compassion, acceptance,** and **gratitude.** When we live from the values of the heart, we live with more **peace, purpose,** and **happiness.** Resting on this foundation of the heart, we are then able to reach out in love towards others spreading peace and healing into the world.

The only way to heal our world and take care of our future generations is to heal ourselves in the present. My aspiration and hope is that we can reconnect with our own heart space and use its wisdom to heal ourselves, and in turn, heal the world. This book is the mindful process that I went through on my own healing journey. It is a culmination of what I learned from all of my teachers from great Buddhist monks to the animals in the forest. My hope is that it will give the reader a tangible process to follow for their own healing making a deep mindfulness practice accessible to all.

The healing journey is not without effort, trial, and resistance. There are many lessons that I return to daily reworking the places that I get stuck or forgetful. I walk my clients through the same process adapting the steps to their personal journey but following the same essential foundation. This intentional healing journey is a practice that becomes a lifestyle, and this lifestyle will heal you and the world around you. Only we can transform the uncertainty of the world into peace, and that transformation begins with a mindful look inward.

PART 1

Coming Back Home

Healing comes from stillness. When a deer is injured, he does not continue to travel and forage. He finds a comfy, safe place within the trees and lies still until he is healed. In our constant need for progress and forward motion, we have lost the ability to come back home and heal. We are unable to be still long enough to hear what our illness really needs and how to nurture it. When we are hurt or ill, we immediately reach outward to doctors, drugs, and vices to fix us so that we can continue our incessant movement, but we have not really heard or healed the root problem. We have mended a symptom and left the internal wound unheard. True healing comes from a deep understanding of the root cause of suffering, and the only way to understand it is to be present with it. As David Hawkins says, "to really know means to be and thus both subject and knower are unified."[2] In order to know our suffering, we must be one with it, not fight it or run from it, but come back home to it and see that it is us and we are it. We have to come back home in stillness so that we can listen to and understand our hurts, making peace with them so that we find peace within ourselves.

I

Open to Change

Mindfulness

Mindfulness is the foundation for this process of healing because it brings our focus back home to self. It has been described as a state of open mindedness in which one is aware of internal and external stimuli but does not react to them. [3,4] This takes us out of a mode of going, doing, solving, planning, and manipulating back into a mode of being with our experience, in non-judgmental awareness. This non-judging observation of all mental formations generates mental health, cognition, and compassion, which decreases the negative effect of difficult feelings and sensations.[3] Essentially, mindfulness gives us the tools necessary to reconnect with self in peace.

Our experience of life is generated by our mind's interpretation of and reaction to the input it receives. Mindfulness is a means of creating positive, healthy responses to stimuli that empower us rather than enslave us. We give ourselves space from thoughts and messages so that we can observe our programmed reactions, recognize if they help or harm us, and then choose a response that supports our well-being. Mindfulness has been proven to decrease stress, fear response, depression, and anxiety by helping us to slow down our reaction in the limbic system, our center for fight, flight, or freeze, and spend more time processing input in the prefrontal cortex, where we can create more refined responses. We also learn how to live in present moment awareness, spending less time catastrophizing about the future and ruminating about past traumas. We learn to live in gratitude for the experience of life instead of constantly trying to change, manipulate, and fix.

When I first began with the practice, I found it nearly impossible to sit in stillness for five minutes. My mind and body were used to being busy all the time running here and there, never listening to what was really going on within me. To sit in stillness was uncomfortable because I had so many unidentified fears and unsolved traumas lurking within me. I thought that if I stopped moving, I would be swallowed up in all their darkness. What I failed to realize is that the anxious feelings were created by my aversion to these experiences rather than the actual experience itself. I felt like I was running from a big scary monster because I was stuck in my fear response; I was allowing it to grow within me rather than stopping and looking back to see that what I was really running from was a tiny field mouse. Most of our fears are created within our own minds and our aversion to them fuels their growth. If we could simply sit still and invite them in, we would see that they are just harmless messengers trying to tell us something important about our healing.

Mindfulness gave me the tools to stop running; then I could turn around and look at what was chasing me. I subsequently found that the only reason it had been scary was because I had allowed it to grow within the shadows of my mind for so long. When the light shone on it, it shrank down to a manageable mouse. This process does not happen overnight, and sometimes our traumas are too big to sit with right away. That's why we need to approach the practice delicately. We may start with very basic exercises and then work our way up to sitting with our traumas. The best way to start a mindfulness practice is by sitting with the breath.

The breath is the foundation of a mindfulness practice. It is a tool that is always present and available when we need to take a mindful pause. It is what grounds us into an observing and reflecting state. The breath brings us peace on a philosophical level because when we connect with the breath, we are reminded of the miracle of life and how amazing our body is in allowing us to be conscious functioning beings. We recognize that if we are breathing, more is going right in our world than wrong, because we are still able to participate in this miraculous gift of life. The breath also reminds us that we are connected to all living beings who share the same intake and output of these basic elements. We recognize that the same elements that make up our being also make up all of the beings in the world around us. We see that every living being participates in the same process of oxygen exchange, whether it be the intake of oxygen and the output of carbon dioxide or the intake of carbon dioxide and the output of oxygen. This reminds us that we are not alone on this wonderful planet but are in fact interconnected with everything within it.

The breath also has the ability to transition us from our sympathetic nervous system back into our parasympathetic, which allows us to rest and replenish. The diaphragm is connected within the autonomic nervous system by the vagus nerve, which runs through many of our major organs and into our brain. This system is a feedback loop dictating which state of being we are in. When we get feedback from either the mind or the body that we are in a stress state, then we switch into our sympathetic nervous system or the state of fight, flight, or freeze. In this state, our heart rate rises, or pupils dilate, our blood moves out to our muscles and extremities, we turn off our digestive system and our recovery systems, and we turn off our higher cognitive processing. This state is necessary for when we need to save ourselves in a dangerous situation. However, it can deteriorate our health if we stay in it for too long, which is what many of us do when we live our lives in stress.

In order to switch out of this stress state, we need to break the feedback loop somewhere within the autonomic nervous system. It is nearly impossible to alter the state of our digestive system or our heart rate, and in most cases we are not able to stop stress in our mind by simply thinking we are no longer stressed. So, we have to break the stress cycle somewhere, and the breath is the perfect place to start. We have the ability to alter our breathing patterns even when we are stressed. And when the vagus nerve passes by the diaphragm and detects that we are breathing slowly, deeply, and intentionally, it sends a message back to the brain saying that we are in a relaxed state. This begins to break through the stress cycle and switch us back into the parasympathetic nervous system in which we can digest, nourish ourselves, rest our muscles and heart, use our higher thinking processes, and increase our immune defenses.

The breath gives us a safe and calm place to come back to no matter where we are or what we are experiencing.

The following exercises will help you to reconnect with your breath.

1.1.1 BREATHING EXERCISES

Feeling the breath

Place all of your attention on the breath and follow the sensations from where the air enters your nose to how it fills the diaphragm. You may feel that the air is cooler when it enters and warmer when it exits. You may feel the slight movement of the hairs on your upper lip or the slight flare of the nostrils as air passes. You may feel the slight opening of the throat as it allows air to pass or the rise and fall of the chest.

As you pull the air deeper into the body, you may feel the expansion of the stomach and the side ribs and out into the back. You may feel the slight contraction as the belly button pulls back towards the spine and you gently squeeze out any remaining air in the lungs.

Find the place within the process of breathing that holds your attention best and continually bring you focus back to it anytime the mind wanders.

5-5-7 *breathing*

Breathe in for five seconds, hold the breath for five seconds, and breathe out for seven seconds. Pause at the bottom of the exhale and breathe out a little bit more before breathing back in.

Count your breaths

Count each in breath and out breath. Each time that your mind wanders, bring your attention back to the breath and start back at one. This is done in non-judgment. We do not judge when the mind wanders; we gently guide it back to the breath.

The second step in the art of mindfulness is to become an observer. Once all of the distractions have settled, you can begin connecting with the world around you on a deeper level. When you look with mindful eyes, you see the beauty in all things. You see how they are all connected and how they all play a crucial part in the bigger system. You find joy in the things that usually go unnoticed.

A teacher once told me her story of being able to look mindfully. She was suffering from depression and struggled to connect with the beauty around her. Every morning she would walk by the same cherry blossom tree that used to bring her so much joy but she just couldn't feel it. She was too trapped in her own mind. So she made a conscious decision that every time she walked by the tree she would stop and really look. Whether or not she felt the joy, she would spend a few breaths simply taking in the tree and really seeing it. After a few months of doing this every day, one day she was looking at the tree and the joy returned. She could once again connect with the awe-inspiring beauty of the outside world.

You can use the following exercises to become a mindful observer.

1.1.2 EXERCISES ON BECOMING A MINDFUL OBSERVER

Observe a flower

Sit in front of a flower and observe its every detail. Allow the flower to become the most important thing in your reality. Notice every fold, every wrinkle, every crack, and crease. Look as though seeing for the first time. The flower is perfect in all its imperfections. It is not trying to be anything but what it is. Every characteristic makes it unique and adapted to its environment.

Observe how the flower is not separate from all of the elements and parts that make it up. Within the flower is the soil, the wind, the sun, the rain and clouds. The flower is the roots, the leaves, the stem, and the pollen. It is connected to all things. See the true nature of the flower.

Be in your surroundings

Sit in a pleasant place and tune into your senses one at a time. Give them your full attention.

Be with the sense of sound. Listen as though you were hearing things for the first time. Don't judge. Don't tell a story. Just listen.

Then tune into your sense of smell. Smell with curiosity.

Then tune into your sense of touch. Don't create new sensations, just pay attention to the ones you already have. Feel the breeze, the hair on your neck, and the fabric on your skin.

Then open your eyes and look as though you were seeing for the first time. Don't judge. Don't name. Just enjoy the shapes, colors, and contrasts.

Be fully present for your surroundings.

In these ways, we can begin our journey back to self by allowing stillness in our life and intentionally connecting with the present moment. Once we find some grounding and stability within the practice, we can use it to look deeper into the nature of our body and mind. We reconnect with those unaddressed wounds and soften to them so that healing can begin.

Neuroplasticity

When we come back home to our mind and body, our motivation lies in understanding. Simply observing our inner workings can tell us a lot about their nature, but a little guidance from neuroscience can clarify the muddy areas. It gives us a deeper understanding of how our contemplative practices are able to transform us. Neuroscience now tells us that the mind is ever changing and adaptable, giving us hope for the possibility of change and transformation.

Until the 1900's, it was believed that we were born with the brains we would have for life, and that after a certain age, we could no longer change them. Neuroplasticity has blown this belief away with the wind. It is now proven that our brains continue to reshape themselves throughout our entire lifespan. We are consistently able to transform our reality, abilities, beliefs, IQ, and even our genes by altering how we process information in our brains. In his book *The Brain That Changes Itself*, Norman Doidge interviews and witnesses the work of many neuroscientists who alter human potential by altering the brain. Individuals have reprogrammed their right brain to perform functions lost in the left brain, cured paralysis caused by stroke, healed OCD habits, eliminated chronic pain, reduced limitations of autism, and cured addiction along with many other amazing feats simply by reprogramming the brain. I shouldn't say "simply," because reprogramming the brain requires an immense amount of awareness, concentration, and effort, motivated by the volition and dedication to make new choices.

This may make some of us uncomfortable because it is easier to blame our bad habits and dysfunctions on things outside of our control. We like to believe that society, circumstance, genetic predisposition, and past experience are what created our discomforts, illnesses, and psychological troubles because then we carry no responsibility. We then search outside of ourselves for solutions, turning to drugs, doctors, and external circumstances to make us feel better. Neuroplasticity proves that healing can be found within ourselves. If we can change how we relate to our experiences, our circumstances, and our genetic differences, then we can change how they manifest in our lives.

Neuroscience tells us that there is nothing within our brain or body too great to be transformed and healed. But in order to change our brain maps we have to be paying attention.[1] That is why mindfulness and neuroscience are inseparable companions. Mindfulness gives us the ability to come back home and pay attention to what is happening within, allowing the brain to reform connections that lead to healing.

PART 2

Healing Ourselves with Kindness

Once we settle into stillness and open ourselves to the possibility of transformation and healing, we can soften to our experiences and be with them in kindness. No healing can occur when we fight against or resist our experiences. Fighting and resisting triggers our stress response, which puts us into our sympathetic nervous system and takes energy away from our replenishing and healing systems. Prolonged stress states decrease our ability to form long-term memories [12], increase the feeling of pain [4], decrease our immune system, lower our ability for cognitive processing [13], and increase our sensitivity to negative emotions. [32] The best way to heal is to step away from our fight with experience and step back into peace and kindness.

Mindfulness helps us to develop compassion for all of our experiences. Instead of trying to change, alter, manipulate, or control what is happening around and within us, we simply observe in non-judgmental awareness. This does not mean that we renounce our desire to improve or progress, it means we stop fighting in order to do it. We make peace with ourselves and the world. We do not need to fight in order to make transformation happen. Transformation happens naturally, as change is the only constant in life. When we step back and rest in peace, the transformation and healing that occurs will be very beautiful and natural, setting us up for a harmonious relationship with the world around us.

For example, when we feel sad, we do not try to fix the problem and end our sadness immediately. We accept that we are feeling sad. We allow it to be present within us and we observe. In these moments of observation, we begin to understand the origination of our reaction to the situation, and we show that hurt part of ourselves compassion, listen to what we need, and set intentions to find the resources available to meet those needs. Now we move through sadness towards healing instead of trying to fight it, deny it, or run from it.

Healing not only needs to happen at the physical level but also the mental and spiritual levels. Our mind, body, and spirit all form a harmonious system, and a problem in one area will lead to a problem in another. Our mental states have the capacity to alter our physical ones, and our spiritual states influence both. The input received by our body is translated into messages that are sent to the spinal cord and brain for interpretation and reaction formation. The emotional and mental state of our brain will affect how the information is interpreted and will change the reaction we create. Our mental states can also send messages to our body, telling it to turn on or off certain systems, leading to physical manifestations based on our mental constructs. There cannot be physical manifestations without mental ones. A spiritual foundation can affect the way we relate to both our physical and mental experiences and change our interpretation of reality. Spiritual endeavor and intention change the brain function and the body's physiology. [24] A strong spiritual practice can lead to a healthy relationship with both mind and body.

Mindfulness helps us to reconnect mind, body, and spirit. By becoming aware of our body and mind, we begin to know the self. As found in the Gospel of Thomas, "Whoever has not known himself has known nothing, but whoever has known himself has simultaneously achieved knowledge about the depth of all things." [43] "And whoever has come to know the depth of all being comes to know himself and discovers his spiritual origin." [35] Our spirituality is found within our own body and mind, and as our spirituality deepens, our whole experience of life becomes spiritual. We see that we are connected to all things and that all things hold the same divine nature. This restores the peace within us and leads to healing of self and the world.

2

Mindful of the Body

We can begin our discovery of self by learning how to listen to the body. When we are not listening, the body gets louder and louder and may develop illness or injury to get us to stop and listen. We have disconnected from our bodies out of necessity. We live in a society that tells us we cannot stop. We cannot stop working, we cannot stop performing, and we cannot stop having fun even if the fun is killing us. The body usually alerts us when we need to take a pause and nurture ourselves, but because we believe that pausing is not possible, we stop listening.

The body holds much wisdom and insight into our wellness, and it wants to be heard. Every cell of our body contains our past stories and wounds. We hold our societal programming within each fiber of our being. By observing the functioning of our body, we learn much about our ancestors, our society, and ourselves. The body can tell us what needs to be healed in all of these areas. The practice begins with us learning how to pay attention to the body.

My path towards listening to the body was a tumultuous one. I traveled through many illnesses and injuries until I was finally willing to listen. In order to become still enough to listen, I had to suffer one herniated disc and one ruptured disc that created nerve damage down the left side of my body. I lost all mobility in my lower back and couldn't even bend forward far enough to spit toothpaste in the sink. My inability to continue moving forced me to come back home and listen. But even through the injury, I spent three years fighting. I simply wanted to get back to "normal," and to not have to pay attention to my body. Only when I accepted that I was not going to go back but had to move forward with a new way of relating to my body was I able to begin healing. Before my injury, I saw my body as something to be used for my own desires. After my injury, I realized that I was not separate from my body and that we had to work together in a harmonious dance. I would listen to its insight and wisdom rather than ordering it around like a tool to be used.

Healing takes place when the mind and body remain in direct communication. The body is not an inanimate object that we can use up and then throw away. It's not a car that we can take into the shop for others to repair and eventually trade in for a newer model. Our body is a reflection of our internal state. It is the physical evidence of how we take care of our mind and spirit. If the body is failing, it is a sign that we need to come back home and begin healing in the mind, body, and spirit. We like to blame all of our unhappiness on our body's inability to do what we want, but most likely we were unhappy before it broke down. We were probably living untrue to our hearts, harming our well-being, and our body failing was the only thing that could get us to pay attention.

In order to listen to the body, we must first learn how to reconnect with it and be still. Paying attention to the body is a learned skill because humans have become very heady beings. We spend a lot of time up in our minds; thinking, planning, strategizing, and telling stories. When our attention is in our mind, we can forget about what we are experiencing in our bodies. We may only notice physical sensation when it becomes so strong that we can't ignore it. It is very important to spend time connecting with the body so that we know what is happening. Often, we can prevent serious illness or injury by noticing warning signs and taking action before it manifests into a major issue. Because we are trained only to pay attention to sensations that are out of the norm, it will take some training to be able to observe what the body is feeling in a normal living state.

You can use these two exercises to help you begin to pay attention to the body.

2.2.1 EXERCISES ON PAYING ATTENTION TO THE BODY

Tuning into our senses

Sit in a quiet peaceful place and allow your mind to settle. Once you are focused inward, clap your hands. Use some force and stiff hands so that you create a strong sensation. Hold the hands about four inches apart and tune all of your awareness to the sensations in them.

Observe with curiosity as though you were experiencing touch for the first time. Try not to label, judge, or tell a story; just feel. Notice if the sensation is different in different spots on the hand.

Then change your focus to just one small spot on one hand. It may be one fingertip or one place in the center of the palm. Place all of your attention here. Notice if the sensation in this one spot is different from the overall sensation in the hand. Does focusing on this one spot change your experience of the sensations elsewhere in the hand?

Now bring your focus back wide and see if you can find the sensation that you felt in that one spot elsewhere in the hands. Begin to observe as the sensation fades away. How is it evolving over time? What sensation is left when the one we created is gone?

Then widen your focus even further. Can you feel the same baseline sensation of aliveness that you found in the hands elsewhere in the body? Maybe this tingling or this vibration of life. This is the feeling of being awake and aware.

Now you can bring your hands together to touch. Really be with the feeling of them touching one another. Does it feel different now than it normally does because you are so aware of it? Play with moving the hand and fingers and feeling every sensation of movement.

Now allow your hands to rest on your lap as they settle back into a normal state, but keep your awareness alive to all of the sensations in your body. This is what it feels like to be connected with sensation.

Body Scan

This is a Body Scan meditation to get you in touch with what is going on in your physical form. You will approach the sensations in your body with open and accepting awareness. You may want to lie down on your back with your knees and head supported by a cushion.

Allow your whole body to relax, giving every muscle permission to stop supporting you as you give your weight over to the earth. You can feel the earth softening beneath you, molding to the weight of your body. You can begin the scan by becoming aware of your internal organs and systems that keep you alive and functioning every day: your lungs, digestive system, detoxing organs, and heart. Send recognition and gratitude to each one.

Then your sense organs, eyes, tongue, ears, nose, and skin. What a miracle to be able to sense the world around us.

Now you can begin your scan of the body, beginning at the feet. Acknowledge each part of the body, identifying with any sensation you find there. Observe without judgment, without telling a story, and without trying to fix. Right now we just notice and realize that every experience, good or bad, is a part of this great gift of being alive.

If your mind gets stuck in areas of tension or pain, use the breath to move it forward onto another part of the body. Travel through the whole body part by part before bringing the whole body into your awareness recognizing that each part is one piece of the integral whole. Reunite the body all together leaving no part out and send gratitude all through it.

Once we are able to connect with the body and its sensations, we develop an open-minded acceptance of all its experiences. It is easy to stay connected with our body when it is healthy and performing in a way that pleases us. However, if our body is sick or hurting, we have a tendency to separate ourselves from our physical form. We say mean things about our body and accuse it of not living up to our standards. Our relationship with the body becomes a Me against It battle; my body is fighting me. This is an absurd but all too real thought pattern. How can we be separate from our physical form? Our body and sense impressions are a large part of why we can experience life. Even if they aren't functioning properly, they are still our connection to the outside world. To divide the body from the "I" is simply impossible. So why do we do it?

It can be easier to disconnect from a suffering body because it allows us to deny the fragility of our physical form. We may feel a sense of safety when removed from the aches and pains that remind us that the body is vulnerable. But suffering does not come from the actual pain or illness, it comes from our resistance to it. As living beings, we will experience pain and illness. There is not one person who has never been sick or injured or died. The feeling that it should not happen to us and that we should always be well causes us much suffering.

There can also be a lot of shame felt when we are sick, injured, or imperfect. Our society tells us that we should have perfect bodies, that we should be healthy at all times, and that if we're not we need to do something about it so that we return to our flawless state as quickly as possible. Because of this stigma around being imperfect, we feel as though we are doing something wrong when we become unwell. Instead of listening to the true needs of the body, we spend a lot of money on elective risky surgeries, non-crucial medications that come with other harmful side effects, and endless treatments promising to make us perfect again. These feelings of guilt and shame only worsen our condition and keep us even further from the true needs of our body. They are like the second arrow of hurt that strikes on top of our already ailing body.

Instead of looking at pain and illness as enemies, try to look at them as messengers of healing. Take a few minutes to write down the major illnesses you have experienced and what reaction you had to them. Then reflect on what you learned from them and how they have shaped who you are. I bet you will find that they gave you some of your most valuable lessons and redirected your life on a meaningful path. Most of our most valuable lessons come from hardships. We can choose to use our experiences as opportunities for growth and connection. Think about what hard experiences you are having now that you can choose to use for growth.

Illness is not something to fight against. It is an opportunity to develop self-compassion and love. If we start a battle against our ailing body, all we are doing is tearing ourselves apart. Make peace with your body and ask it what it really needs to be happy. Healing and growth do not stem from fear and anger. If you are fearful and angry with your illness or injury, then you are not open to learning from it. In order to transform our suffering, we must first accept it and soften to it so that we can listen to it from a place of peace.

We can begin this practice of acceptance by first recognizing the miracle that the body really is. Whether or not we are experiencing pain or injury, we are alive. If we are still able to breathe, then more is going right in our lives than wrong. Life is a gift. To be able to experience and participate in life is an amazing miracle. Reconnect with your gratitude for this miracle. Take your focus away from everything that your body is struggling with and place it back onto what makes life so spectacular. Your body constantly works to keep you alive and well. It wants to be healthy so that it can be in communion with the world. Stop fighting it and allow it to work its magic. Believe in the body's ability to heal.

When we are able to trust the body's ability to heal we get out of our own way. We stop fighting the injury and give it the peace it needs to heal. From this place of trust, we begin to soften to our pain and illness. We take down the barriers between it and the rest of the body welcoming it back into the whole. It is not separate from us. It is a manifestation of our own being and needs the support of our whole being to be healed. When we divide it out of our being and make it the other, we are denying it the healing powers of the body and mind. It is a part of us and we can heal it.

Illness is not the only thing that we judge within the body. Even when the body is healthy, we focus on what needs to be changed or fixed. We tell ourselves things like "I'm too fat," "My nose is too big," or "My skin has too many freckles." This is a very sad way to see the body. The body is a gift from God or the universe, and it should be cherished. By saying that your body is imperfect, you are saying that God or the universe has made a mistake. Do you really believe that? You were made exactly as you were meant to be and you are a beautiful creation. By loving yourself, you are loving God and the universe. You are showing respect for the whole system that created you to be an integral part of it. Accept your body. Love your body. You are exactly as you were meant to be.

The following exercises will help you to soften to your body and accept it.

2.2.2 EXERCISES ON ACCEPTING THE BODY

Seeing the body as a miracle

You can do this exercise following a Body Scan (explained above). Once you are in contact with each part of the body and the body is reunited within your consciousness, begin to give gratitude towards it.

Recognize all of the things that your body does for you. Recognize how it keeps you alive, and how it allows you to connect with the world and act within it. Acknowledge all of the miraculous activities you are able to do.

Understand that in loving the body, you are loving all of creation. In loving the body, you are giving gratitude to life. Know that your body was created for a specific purpose and that you are made in the divine nature. You are divine. In accepting the body, we accept the divine and step into our purpose. Love your body.

Soften to illness and pain

This exercise should also be done after a Body Scan so that you are in contact with each part of the body in non-judgmental awareness. You can then place your attention on the areas of your body where you feel tension, sickness, or pain. If you do not have any physical pain or illness, then identify the areas of the body that you are unhappy with or want to change.

Place a hand over this area of the body. Listen to how you communicate with this area.

What are you saying to it?

How do your words feel?

How does the body react to them?

What are you asking it to do?

How do you see it?

Are you fighting with it?

Are you pushing it away and denying it?

Do you feel any guilt or shame because it is there? Is this really how you want to interact with the body?

What would the body rather hear from you?

Can you see this ailment as an equal part of you?

Now be with the pain, illness, or imperfection in love. See if you can take down the boundaries around the difficult area. Soften around it so that you give it room to breathe and move. See if you can soften its edges so that it is no longer a solid defined object. Allow it to dissipate outwards as you widen your awareness further and further.

As our attention widens, the difficult area seems less dominant.

It melts into the rest of the body, no longer a separate self but included within the whole. The fighting subsides as it is held by the body.

The body can now share its healing energies with itself. Allow the flow of energy to enter into it, washing the pain away and reintegrating it back into the harmonious system.

Now that we are no longer fighting with the body and illness, we can begin to understand its nature. Illness and injury are signals telling us that we are in danger or that something is out of balance within us. The body is trying to protect itself by reacting to these threats. Pain is telling us that we need to protect a certain area of the body from a harmful situation or action. Illness is telling us that we have a foreign invader in our body that needs to be expelled. In a healthy system, the pain and illness are not what need to be fought against. They are friendly messengers and warriors trying to keep us well. We really need to recognize what it is that is triggering these defense reactions and remedy those. By listening to the body and how it is reacting to our surroundings, activities, and consumption, we can learn how to better take care of ourselves so that illness and injury don't need to manifest.

The problem is that we don't want to listen to the body. It

is hard to listen to the body when it is telling us that we need to be under less stress, change our diet, stop consuming harmful toxins, find more time for self-care, and do gentle exercise. These are messages of changes that many of us have become really good at ignoring, because we live in a society that requires us to keep going even if our bodies are telling us to slow down. Whether we are struggling with a job with demanding hours, a home life that requires constant attention, or our concept of play that keeps us pushing the limits, life encourages us to pursue success over health and immediate pleasures over long-term well-being. And we learn to ignore or cover up the warning signs from our bodies so that we don't miss out or disappoint. This short term answer to get our to-do lists done may be causing long term harm to our well-being.

It is very important to recognize the techniques we use to tune out the messages from our body. Otherwise we will continue consuming and doing the things that bring us pleasure in the moment as our body manifests more and more illness and injury until we finally hit a breaking point. We usually turn away from the true messages of the body by abusing substances, overeating, over-engaging with media and television, distracting ourselves with social engagements or shopping, over-exercising, or working. These are some of the ways that we use the body to keep ourselves distracted from the truth of our internal state rather than being with the body in compassionate listening.

Although the lifestyle changes that the body may be asking for are hard to make, the rewards that they offer far outweigh the initial effort. It is just like when you start a new sport. At first, everything hurts and you want to give up because it's new and hard, but after a month, you start to see improvement. Your body is firmer and more agile. You are lighter on your feet. You have more energy throughout the day and your mind is clearer. Then, because you are so happy with the results and because your improvement has made the sport more enjoyable, you actually look forward to doing it. It no longer feels like a chore. The same is true for lifestyle changes. At first, all you can see are the things you are giving up—the immediate pleasures that you are denying yourself and the activities you are missing out on. But after you begin to experience the peace and healing that occurs in your mind and body, you no longer see it as an effortful sacrifice. You rest into the new lifestyle with ease and enjoyment, basking in the wellness it provides.

When we understand the potential to live a healthy and balanced life, listening to what the body is asking us to do becomes much easier. The body knows what it needs to be healthy, you just have to be willing to listen. A good place to start is to recognize what limitations the pain or illness is causing you. These limitations are probably what you need to learn about in order to honor your body in a healthy way. For example, a back injury is forcing you to find stillness. This may be because you need to learn how to bring more stillness into your life in a healthy way. The following exercises will help you to notice the ways you disconnect from your body when you don't want to hear its message. They will help you to stay with the body even through discomfort. Listen to what it's asking you to do in order to find more balance and wellness in your life.

2.2.3 EXERCISES ON STAYING WITH THE BODY

Observing the ways we disconnect

It is best to start this exercise with a body scan so that you become connected to the whole body.

Once you are connected with the whole body, imagine a time when you were beginning to feel discomfort in the body and you knew that the body was trying to tell you something that it needed that you felt you could not provide.

What did you do instead of listening?

Where do you turn when you can't hear the pain of the body?

Do you turn to drugs or alcohol?

Do you turn to adrenaline and adventure?

Do you turn to social outlets or media distractions?

Where do you go when you're too uncomfortable to listen?

What are you unwilling to hear?

Why are you unwilling to hear it?

What can't you let go of?

Now imagine yourself staying with the body. Don't turn to your distraction. Find your grounding in the breath. Know that you can hear whatever it has to present and stay with it.

Listening to the body

This exercise can be done after the previous exercise or on its own. Start with a short body scan.

Once you are connected with the body, open your heart and mind to listening to it. Ask the body which areas need to be heard. You may want to place a hand on that area.

Tell it that you are here for it and that you want to listen to what it is trying to say.

As you begin to listen, notice if you have any resistance, and then center back on the breath and stay there. You are grounded and centered enough to hear whatever the body has to say. Ask the body why it hurts.

What does it need from you or the world?

How can you support it?

What needs to change?

How can you nurture it?

Notice the limitations or changes the illness is forcing on you.

Is it making you be more still?

Not consume certain foods or substances?

Not engage in certain activities?

Create more space in your life?

Spend more time alone in self-care?

Reach out for connection and assistance?

Whatever it is that the body forces you to do through the pain or illness is what you need to learn how to do in a balanced way in order to heal.

Imagine yourself able to meet all of these needs of the body. Notice as it softens just by being heard.

Tell the body that you have intentions of trying to live in a way that keeps it healthy and happy. Set those intentions for yourself.

Once we're able to stay with the body and listen, we need to understand where our limitations come from and how to move past them. In an imbalanced body and mind, pain and illness can be a manifestation of past fears or stories that keep us ill long past the presence of the actual threat or intrusion. In these situations, most of our suffering comes from the added story we tell ourselves that is locked into our memory.

Pain is formed by a gathering of evidence from many sources before the brain determines how much of a reaction to create. How much pain we feel is determined in significant part by our brains and minds, our current mood, our past experiences of pain, our psychology, and how serious we think our injury is.[12] If our past fears and experiences of injury send evidence that there is potential for harm, even benign movements can create pain. A heightened emotional state during injury can prolong and strengthen pain responses. Prolonged stress states reduce our ability to heal and may lead to chronic pain and injury. An unhealthy brain can enhance and prolong injury to the body. For this reason, it is very important to recognize how we are relating to pain and injury and trust in our ability to heal so that we don't remain stuck in our injury.

It has been found that a patient's experience of pain originating from an injury or ailment can persist long after the underlying cause has been resolved.[4] This is because pain is created in the brain and projected onto the body. When pain receptors have been hyper sensitized, they fire incessant false alarms, making us believe that the problem is in our body when really it is in our mind.[12] Pain is meant to prevent us from motions that could cause us harm. When we are injured, pain receptors are more sensitive, encouraging us to stop motion in that area. But sometimes our fear around the sensation compounds the pain reaction and we begin to feel pain even before we perform a potentially harmful motion. The brain may get so efficient at preventing us from moving that it includes the motor response in the pain circuit, triggering pain as soon as we have an intent to move.[12]

The mind can also create limitations that don't actually exist in the body. Loss of motion after a stroke can be due to a learned belief that we can't use that part of the body after its control center was damaged in the brain. If we were to believe in the possibility of movement and slowly add motion back, the brain would actually reorganize itself and find a new way to perform the lost function using other brain maps.[12] Nicole Van Ruden, who was paralyzed from chemo treatments that affected her spine, was able to recover mobility by not allowing herself to believe she couldn't. She started with very basic skills and then worked her way up to normal functionality. She says "Your whole mind-set can shift about what you are able to do by simply believing that you can." [12] Our change in belief about limitation can greatly decrease it or eliminate it altogether.

Our susceptibility to illness is much higher when we do not have a healthy balance in our mind and body. When we have high levels of daily stress, we are more likely to experience health problems like the flu, sore throat, headaches, and backaches.[11] There is also a link between our past mental health and our current physical health. Mental health has a direct and indirect effect on physical health, mostly linked to our engagement in physical activity and positive social interactions.[17] Our mental health also affects our ability to heal. When we are in an emotionally triggered state, we shift into our sympathetic nervous system and energy is taken away from healing and replenishing. So the more we worry and become depressed about being sick or injured, the longer we will stay that way and the more susceptible we will be to injury and illness in the future.

The remedy is to treat our illness or injury with kindness. Don't go into an emotionally charged state of fear and resistance. Find peace by changing your mental response. Trust your body's ability to heal and allow it to work its magic. Stop getting in its way! Your body wants to be healthy and whole; we just have to listen to what it needs and comply. Mindfulness and meditation have been found to increase body vitality while decreasing bodily pain and limitations caused by compromised physical health.[7] This is because mindfulness and meditation allow you to make peace with your body and step out of your stress state. They help you to get in tune with what your body needs and respond accordingly. Only when we are at peace with the body and willing to listen to its needs can we heal.

The following exercises will help you to examine your relationship with illness and injury and express kindness to them so that you are better able to heal.

2.2.4 EXERCISES ON EXPRESSING KINDNESS TOWARDS ILLNESS AND INJURY

Recognizing our story around illness or pain

Please begin this exercise with a body scan connecting with the whole body. Find the areas of the body that trouble you. If you do not have any physical pain or illness, then identify the areas of the body that you are unhappy with or want to change.

Place a hand over this area of the body. Listen to the story you tell yourself about this ailment, injury or imperfection.

Are you feeding the fear story?

Are you generating more limitations for yourself by telling limiting stories? Do you hold negative energy in this area by labeling it as bad or unfixable? Are you fearful of making certain movements?

Do you tell yourself not to do certain things because they may make things worse?

Is there stress stored here?

Are these stories helping you heal?

Can you let go of these negative stories?

Can you replace them with an attitude of peace and acceptance?

Notice what this does for your relationship to this part of the body. You may tell it something like, "I know that you are hurting. I'm here for you. I know that there are many things you are still capable of and I am grateful to you. I am here to support you in whatever ways you need."

Notice how you can begin to love it again and notice how love is the first step to healing.

Trusting the body's ability to heal

This exercise can follow the previous one or can be done on its own after a body scan. Find the areas of the body that trouble you. If you do not have any physical pain or illness, then identify the areas of the body that you are unhappy with or want to change.

Place a hand over this area of the body.

What is the body asking for?

How does it need to be nurtured?

Working from your heart space, offer the body what it needs. Allow the difficult area back into the whole body so that it is connected into the whole. Identify with the body's ability to heal.

Listen to the body's deepest desire to be whole and healthy. Trust that the body can heal. Encourage the body to heal.

Tell the body that you are here to help it heal itself. Visualize the body healing itself, reconstructing, rewiring, clearing, cleansing, and detoxing.

Believe that the body can heal. Visualize the body healing for as long as you can, as many times a day as you can. Offer healing energies throughout the entire body.

Stay with the belief that the body can heal. Offer love to the body.

We may be experiencing pain or illness in the body because we have deeper needs within our emotional and spiritual body that aren't getting the attention they're seeking. Unheard messages from our mental, emotional, and spiritual selves manifest as physical ailments because that is often the only form of distress signal we recognize and are comfortable with feeling. If we are able to recognize these messages before they manifest into physical form, then we can sustain a state of well-being. Often these messages are related to the need to attain more safety, security, stability, love, belonging, acceptance, and nurturing.

Because our society has become so averse to authentic emotional and spiritual sharing and support, many people reach out for support in the only way that is acknowledged, physical pain and illness. When we are experiencing physical ailments that can be seen and diagnosed, people pay attention. This is contrary to when we have an aching spirit or heart and are left with no one to turn to. Many people will continue experiencing pain and injury because they are craving empathy and nurturing. The only way that they can receive it is if they are physically unwell. For this reason, it is important to listen to the actual needs of our body, mind, and spirit and then recognize all the resources we have for meeting those needs without having to develop a physical ailment in order to gain access to compassion and empathy.

Developing consistent sources of nurturing and love in our lives can drastically decrease the occurrence of physical ailments.

We can begin by allowing the emotional and spiritual bodies to express themselves. If we already have an ailment, then it is one hundred percent certain that there are emotions held within it. These can be emotions from before the ailment that accumulated when not allowed to be expressed, and then they stuff themselves into the body forming pain. These emotions can also be the emotional experience that built up during the injury or illness. There is no denying that when our body is hurting, so is our mind and spirit, even if it's just because of the adjustments we have to make while being unwell. A hurting body causes us to lose many of the activities and joys in life that we love most. We can feel alone in our suffering and we can feel a lack of support. As we discussed in the previous section, we may also feel self-judgment and anger for being unwell. All of these emotional experiences need just as much love as our physical ailment. We can begin by finding safe places filled with love and acceptance where we can express them, reassuring them that we want to hear them and we want to nurture them.

As we find peace in the body, healing will begin. But in order for healing to last, we have to find balance and peace in mind, body, and spirit. The symptoms felt within the body are a manifestation of what is happening in the mind and spirit. If our body heals, but our mind and spirit remain ill, then the illness will return again and again. To maintain wellness, we must heal our whole selves on a deeper level.

2.2.5 UNDERSTANDING THE EMOTIONAL, MENTAL, AND SPIRITUAL MESSAGES OF OUR BODY

Recognizing our true needs

Please begin this exercise with a body scan connecting with the whole body. Find the areas of the body that trouble you. If you do not have any physical pain or illness, then identify the areas of the body that you are unhappy with or want to change.

Place a hand over this area of the body.

Tell them that you are listening.

Tell them that you want to hear what they really need.

Tell them that you want to offer them the nurturing that they need.

Ask them over and over what it is that they really need.

The answer may morph and change through the session.

Keep asking until the deeper need is revealed.

This need will most likely not be related to the body at all but will be linked to more stability, safety, acceptance, peace, love, compassion, empathy, belonging, etc.

Now look into your life and recognize all the places where these are already accessible. Notice the resources you have for experiencing them.

Set intentions for how you are going to actively engage with these resources so that you can nurture yourself and meet your true needs.

Tell the body thank you for sharing the message and that your intentions are to continue listening so that you can nurture your mind, body, and spirit and begin to heal.

3

Mindful of the Mind

The mind is not just the brain. It is the interconnected system of all of our sense organs, our digestive system, our intuition, our visceral system, and our respiratory system. It is the intelligence that runs all through our body and brain and everything is included within it. Without the input from the body, the brain would have no way of perceiving the world. The brain perceives because the body feels. The amazing thing about the brain is its capacity to interpret and respond to the input received by the body. Without the brain, we would remain in the oversimplified and limiting system described in behaviorism where there is an external stimulus and a programmed reaction with no cognitive ability to process or alter that reaction. But, because the brain is involved, we have the ability to choose how we see the world and form responses that are most likely to generate desired outcomes. We are not stuck on a reaction loop. We will go into further detail on how input is received and processed when we talk about consumption. For now, let's focus on the content of the brain, this place where almost all of the input gets sent and is formed into thoughts, responses, and memories.

As mentioned at the beginning of the book, the brain has the ability to rewire itself, a process known as neuroplasticity. This means that we are always capable of reprogramming how we interpret input and create responses. That's great news! It means that you aren't stuck with unwanted habits and thought patterns. Mindfulness and other contemplative practices help us to transform the brain by allowing us to observe it and understand how it works. This way, we can see our unhealthy patterns and find a way out of them.

As stated by Lao Tzu, "watch your beliefs they become your thoughts, watch your thoughts they become your words, watch your words they become your actions, watch your actions they become your habits, watch your habits they become your character, your character it becomes your destiny."[30] Our destiny is determined by our beliefs, which become our thoughts. What we allow to manifest in our minds will determine who we are and what we do in the world. This is both empowering and intimidating. Empowering because we hold within ourselves the ability to transform our world. Intimidating because not many of us actually know how to be stewards of our own minds leaving us vulnerable to creating a world based on the influences of others. Spend a moment contemplating what David Cuschieri said: "The mind is a powerful force. It can enslave us or empower us. It can plunge us into the depths of misery or take us to the heights of ecstasy.

Learn to use the power wisely."[10] Is your mind enslaving you or empowering you?

In order for the mind to empower us, we have to know how it works. As we begin to investigate the nature of the mind, we find that it spends only fifty percent of the time consciously engaged in the present moment. The other fifty percent of the time it is checked out from the real world and engaged in what is called "mind wandering." This is possible because most of the activities that we do in the day are performed on automaticity, meaning we are capable of doing them because we have programmed motor systems to do so.[32] This is a good thing because if we had to consciously invest in each action like putting on our pants or entering a car we would be very limited on how much we could do in a day. The problem with our ability to perform most tasks without conscious awareness is that our mind is left with a lot of free time to wander and create stories.

With awareness we can choose how to engage with this free mental space. We could place our attention on thoughts and ideas that empower us, or we could place our attention on those that enslave us into destructive mindsets. Unfortunately, it is found that ninety percent of the time our mind spends wandering is dedicated to negative thoughts. These could be thoughts of worry, regret, anger, or judgment.[37] All of this means that most of our minds are actually enslaving us in unhealthy thought patterns. In order to rewire our brain away from negative thinking, we have to learn how to pay attention. We cannot change a pathway if we are not consciously aware of it. [12]

Becoming aware of what we are thinking is a developed skill that takes practice. Mindfulness has been found to increase our awareness of unconscious processes and enables us to redirect our attention back to the present moment. Consequently, we have more cognitive control over what we do and say. [8] We are able to notice when our mind is wandering off into its stories, predictions, and ruminations, and then redirect it to the present moment so that we can be consciously engaged with what we are doing and who we are with. This helps us to engage less with negative thought patterns and increases our enjoyment of and participation in the present moment.

I often use the example of a snow globe. The clear water is that natural open state of the mind. This is the state we want to be in so that we can look through the mind and perceive exactly what is right in front of us, whether it be a task we are tending to or a person we are engaging with. The sparkles in the snow globe are all of the thoughts and stories that dance around in our heads, distracting us from the present moment. These can be regrets, resentments, or longings for the past. They can also be desires and expectations for the present, or worries, excitements, and to do's for the future. Whatever they are, they make it very difficult for us to see clearly in the present moment. Mindfulness is the process of holding the snow globe still long enough for all of these sparkles to settle, leaving that clear open state of mind that allows us to really see the present and engage with it intentionally.

We can begin by stepping back from our thoughts and observing them so that we know where our attention lies. We can identify our thoughts rather than participating in them. This allows us to recognize our thoughts and how they are affecting us. We can then choose where to place our attention. We then discover that we are not our thoughts. Our thoughts are mental manifestations within us, but they are not our ultimate reality and don't have to define our experience of life.

You can begin to recognize the nature of your thoughts with the following exercises.

2.3.1 EXERCISES ON OBSERVING THE MIND

Watching thoughts

You should begin with a simple breathing exercise, coming back to the breath and allowing it to settle your mind and relax your body.

Once you are centered and calm, take your awareness up into your mind. Create a wide open space in the mind. You may imagine it as an open field with soft grasses and a clear blue sky overhead.

Recognize this as the natural state of the mind: open, non-judgmental, and observing. From this place of peace, begin to watch your thoughts as though they were clouds drifting through the sky.

Know that your thoughts, just like the clouds, are all made of the same elements that come together in a certain way for a specific moment and then shift, transform, and disappear as the elements change form.

Your thoughts, like the clouds, are never permanent. They come and go, shift and change. The only thing that remains constant is the natural state of the clear blue sky behind them, open and observing everything that manifests in non-judgmental awareness.

Notice how the clouds manifest into different shapes and sizes. Some are light and wispy, barely holding a shape. Others are bright and attractive like the clouds of a sunset. Some are fluffy and friendly, fun to look at, and creative. Some are dark and scary, enveloping the whole sky and seemingly all encompassing. But no matter what their shape, they all have one thing in common: they will change, transform, move on, and eventually disappear.

Your thoughts are the same. They are different in content but the same in nature. Even the darkest of thoughts will eventually soften and dissipate into rain or into clear sky. No mental state lasts forever.

We find comfort in their impermanence and ever-changing nature. We can allow them to manifest and exist without grasping to them or pushing them away. They will come and go naturally as we rest back in peace.

Noticing where the mind goes

You can begin with a breathing exercise and then step into that clear open space behind thought.

From this space of non-judgmental awareness, begin to watch your thoughts and where they go. Watch as they manifest and then watch your urge to give them importance and follow them away.

Instead of following the thought, just label it; past, present, or future. Notice if it was in the past, the present, or the future. Continue this way for a minute.

Once you feel that you are able to watch the thoughts without following them, you can begin to notice what reaction the thought produces. Watch the thought, know if it is in the past, present, or future, and then name what it brings up in you; anxiety, the need to do, urgency, peace, love, sadness, or blaming.

Don't judge these reactions, just notice that the thought is generating them within you. Instead of following the thought and the reaction it produces, come back to your breath and that open space.

Your thought was of that nature, but you are of the nature of open space and peace. See the difference between your state and the state of your thoughts. They are not the same. Allow your thoughts to continue coming and going as you rest in that peaceful space.

Now that we know that our thoughts are not direct

replications of reality, we begin to explore the freedom to create our own. As Victor Frankl says, "your freedom lies in the space that exists between stimulus and reaction."[19] That space is where thought has the ability to either enslave us or empower us. If you noticed that your thoughts were producing negative reactions, then change your thoughts to create positive reactions. That is the power of the mind. But as Gandhi pointed out, we cannot change our thoughts before changing our beliefs.

The educated mind is one that remains open and available for new ideas, ready to change and adapt to new situations. By staying in tune with nature and the external world, we can find new and innovative ways to interact with it, creating a harmonious, ever-changing reality. An inflexible mind creates beliefs and perspectives from its own subjective reality and then aims to verify them by changing the world to fit into those beliefs. This activity leads cultural groups to try and impose their view of the world on other cultures.[12] The more we forcefully change the world around us to fit our erroneous beliefs, the more we create social environments that confirm the misbeliefs. [39] Essentially, we begin to shape our reality with our own beliefs. This leaves us vulnerable to acting and connecting in ways that align with old, erroneous beliefs rather than observing what our current situation is calling for. If we keep an open mind and observe what the world needs, we can act and connect in ways most beneficial to our well-being.

The way out of this harmful attachment to our own beliefs is to expose ourselves to as many different experiences as possible. As John Taylor Gatto says, "the educated mind is the connected mind, connected to all manner of different human styles, connected to all sorts of complex experiences, some of them fraught with psychological and physical peril, connected to a dizzying profusion of intellectual ideas which interconnect with one another. Most of all the educated mind is connected to itself. Knowing yourself is the foundation for everything else.[20] By coming in contact with difference, we give ourselves the opportunity to understand the world from varying perspectives and in varying contexts. We can then use this information to create a broader version of reality and healthier ways of relating to it.

Contact with different opinions and lifestyles also allows us a deeper look into our own selves. When we realize that not everyone thinks like us or sees the world like us, we are given an immense freedom to reexamine our own beliefs. We see that we are not trapped in our own views and perspectives, but can choose how we want to experience reality. We become more mentally flexible, welcoming new ideas that may serve us better than old programmed ones. This gives us the power of adaptability, which will keep us alive and well in an ever-changing world.

By actively observing the world rather than forcing our beliefs onto it, we can see what it really is rather than what we want it to be. This involves us in a harmonious communion with life rather than a dominion over it. When we try to dominate and control others or our environment, we are acting on our own erroneous beliefs that may not be the most beneficial to us or the planet. By putting down our need to be right, our need to know, our need to control, and surrendering to be guided by the life around us, we see, act, and contribute in ways that lead to true healing.

You can use the following exercises to become aware of your beliefs and open to new ones.

2.3.2 EXERCISES ON DEVELOPING A FLEXIBLE MIND

Is this true?

You can begin with a breathing exercise and then step into that clear open space behind thought.

Begin to observe your thoughts.

Notice which thoughts are loudest for you today.

Notice what reactions they are creating in you and what emotions are behind those reactions.

Now ask yourself, "is this true?"

Continue this for a few minutes, consistently noticing thought and then asking, "is this true?"

As you continue asking, you will notice that your belief in the thought gets weaker.

Who says it's true?

Where did you hear that belief for the first time?

What perspective of the world is that thought based on? Is that perspective true?

Slowly, we become more and more open and less attached to our thoughts and views.

Widening perspective

You can begin with a breathing exercise and then step into that clear open space behind thought.

Begin to notice your thoughts and the beliefs behind them. You can imagine one of those beliefs written on a piece of paper in front of you.

Notice how when you hold it really close to you, it becomes all that you can see. It becomes the lens through which you see the world.

Notice how with it in front of you, you cannot see what's actually around you.

Now hold that belief back and widen your perspective. Open your range of sight up further and further. You can imagine yourself in any natural setting that you would like: mountains, beach, or meadow.

Notice that the more you allow into your sight, the more you are able to see. Watch how everything within nature is constantly changing—coming and going, transforming, and adapting.

Notice how nature does not hold on to one state or one truth. She allows everything to continue flowing and adapting, dying away, and beginning anew.

Allow your beliefs to do the same. And as your context gets larger and larger, begin to imagine other social groups outside of your own.

Ask how do they see this?

Then imagine other cultures and countries and ask, how do they see this? Then step back and take the perspective of Mother Earth looking down on all of us and ask, how does she see this?

And then you can take your perspective even wider, out in space into the whole universe and ask, how does the cosmos see this?

Now your own belief does not seem so big and important. Maybe it no longer seems true at all.

Now that we have opened ourselves up to seeing the world differently, we can begin to reform our thoughts so that they empower us. We know that thoughts have the ability to change who we are and the world that we are in. When you actively visualize yourself carrying out an action, the same neural pathways are being activated as if you were actually performing the task.[12] This means that the more you think about something, the more those neural pathways are strengthened within the brain, making you more likely to act that way in the future. If we want to make a change in our lives, we have to start by believing we can and then visualizing the possibility.

In the same way, if we want the world to be a positive place, then we have to start by believing it is. If we want to manifest more of something in our lives, then the best place to start is to notice all the ways in which it already shows up. This will automatically increase its presence in our lives. If you want more love, then focus on all the ways love already shows up in your life and pour your energy into them. If you want more peace, then focus on all the ways peace already shows up in your life and pour your energy into them. If you want more abundance, then place your attention on all the ways abundance already shows up in your life. All that we need is already present in our world, we just have to notice it and engage with it.

We can also change our world simply by changing the way we see it. Ninety percent of our happiness has to do with the way our brain processes the world, not with what is actually in the world.[1] Our reality is created by how we interpret and process the input we receive based on past experiences and memories that have trained us how. Much of this process is happening without our conscious awareness.[32] So in order for us to change how we see the world, we have to consciously develop new ways of interpreting stimuli. If you notice that a perception or a viewpoint is causing you anger, discomfort, or other negative reactions, then ask yourself, is this perception true? How could I relate differently to this situation? Every experience is exactly what you need in order to become who the world needs you to be, so use them wisely.

I find it especially helpful to see all experiences and

interactions as a teaching tool. Instead of taking an experience personally, I step back and ask myself, what is this trying to teach me? How can I use this to grow and transform? This way, I do not feel offended or attacked by my experiences, but helped. I cannot always do this in the moment. Occasionally I do take things personally and I do react out of self-protection. When this happens, once things have calmed down, I take a moment to be with my experience and reflect so that I can learn from it. I understand that this too belongs and was a crucial step along my journey. I try not to judge or condemn my actions, but learn from them.

The world never gives you more than you can handle. As long as you can remain present for everything that you experience, knowing that what's right in front of you is the most important thing in the world. Then you will have the patience and understanding to learn and grow from all things. As Jon Kabat Zinn says, "Meditation is seeing things clearly and deliberately positioning yourself in relationship to them." [27] Choose the relationship you want to have with the world and manifest the reality you want to have.

You can use the following exercises to develop healthy thought patterns that help you create the world you want to live in.

2.3.3 EXERCISES ON CREATING A HEALTHY RELATIONSHIP WITH EXPERIENCE

Reconstructing the thought wheel

You can begin with a breathing exercise to become present and connected. You will then step into that open space behind thought so that you can observe your thoughts without becoming engaged with them.

Notice their ever-changing nature. Find comfort in their impermanence. Pay attention to what thoughts continue to arise for you.

Notice how it is very rare for you to have a novel thought. They almost always repeat themselves over and over and are generated from something you heard or witnessed before.

You can imagine this cycle of thought like the wheel of fortune. You spin it around and land on different thoughts, but most of the thoughts on the wheel stay the same. Begin to notice the nature of the thoughts on your wheel.

Do most of them cause positive or negative reactions within you?

You can pick one of your thoughts to focus on.

When did you begin thinking this way?

What perception of the world is this thought based in?

What perception of self is this thought based in?

Does this thought create the reality that I want to live in?

If not, then begin to transform the thought. Ask yourself, how could I see this differently?

How do I want to see the world?

How do I want to see myself?

How do I want to see this situation?

What thought would create the reality I want to live in?

You can continue in this way for the other thoughts on your wheel of fortune, until when you spin the wheel, each thought that you could possibly land on is one that creates the world you want to live in.

Developing a healthy relationship with experience

You can begin with a breathing exercise to become present and connected. You will then step into that open space behind thought so that you can observe your thoughts without becoming engaged with them. Find comfort in the impermanence of all mind states. They manifest, present themselves, transform, and fade away—always changing.

This reminds us that we don't have to take any one thought or mind state too seriously. Imagine a current situation in your life that you are resisting or struggling with.

Notice your relationship to it. Listen to your thoughts about it. Listen to your thoughts about self, the other, and the world.

What reaction are these thoughts creating in you?

What are they doing to your body and your mind?

Who are you being when you have them?

Is this who you want to be?

What reality are you living in when you have these thoughts?

Is this the reality you want to live in?

Begin to loosen your grasp on these mindsets and thoughts. They don't have to be your reality. Feel your body soften. Feel your mind open.

How do you want to see this situation and the world?

How do you need to relate to this situation so that you can be the person you want to be?

How do you need to relate to this situation so that you can live in the world you want to live in?

Create the thoughts that best serve you and continue to repeat them to yourself.

As we reprogram how we interpret the input from the world, we begin to realize our potential to create our own reality. Deepak Chopra says, "When you begin to suspect that you are the author of your own existence, seeking has begun. When you start to use your awareness to actively shape your life, seeking has brought you an answer. When you look around and know reality is based entirely on consciousness, seeking has reached its goal."[9] Our reality is the experience of our own interpretation of life, and in our ability to shape our interpretation lies our freedom to create our own reality. What reality do you want to live in?

Thich Nhat Hanh explains that "The kingdom of God is available to you in the here and the now. But the question is whether you are available to the kingdom. Our practice is to make ourselves ready for the kingdom so that it can manifest in the here and the now. You don't need to die in order to enter the kingdom of heaven. In fact, you have to be truly alive in order to do so."[22] He is saying that your consciousness can manifest the kingdom of God in the here and now if you engage with life in mindful awareness. When we see life in deep awareness, we engage with the miracle of its true nature and we experience the kingdom of God on Earth.

In order to engage with life in this way, we must free ourselves of our harmful and destructive thought patterns and open to direct experience of what is. Instead of telling stories about what we experience, labeling, judging, and manipulating, we simply experience in open-minded awareness. We look with the eyes of a curious child marveling at the wonders of life, ready to learn and grow from each experience. This is true joy. When we are aware of the wonders of life at every moment. And this type of awareness manifests the kingdom of God in the here and now.

As you are washing the dishes, watch where your mind goes.

Are you telling stories about all the things you have to do next, about how you are always the one who has to wash the dishes, or how you are sick of doing so many chores? Or are you engaging with the miracles of life before your eyes? Are you seeing the miraculous way that water arrives in your faucet? Are you noticing the miracle of the warm water trickling over your hands? Are you looking out the window and seeing the bird singing on a branch? Are you feeling the sun rays gently caressing your face? Wherever your mind goes is the reality you are living. If you are living an awful reality, it's because your mind is creating it; it's time to engage with a different story.

All over Thich Nhat Hanh's practice center, Plum Village, there are little reminders of the miracles of life. At the sink, there is a reminder to recognize the miracle of water dropping from the clouds, running down the mountains and rivers, and eventually arriving in your faucet. Next to the toilet there is a reminder that the body is a miraculous thing, processing our food, giving us nutrients, and expelling the waste. Over the light switch there is a reminder that light comes from the energy provided by the sun and stored in batteries to travel through wires to arrive at the light bulb. Everywhere, you are reminded to really look at what is being offered to you in each simple comfort. When we look at life with this deep awareness, there is no other option than to feel gratitude, peace, and love.

2.3.4 EXERCISES ON CREATING THE KINGDOM OF GOD

Watching your story

You can begin with a breathing and centering exercise. Bring your attention back to self, back to this present moment.

Imagine yourself in the middle of an activity that you do daily. Notice your surroundings, what you are doing, and what you are saying.

Now look into your mind and notice what story you are telling yourself about this situation.

What always or never statements are you making?

What are you engaging with?

Are you present for your surroundings?

Are you present for the people you are with?

Are you present for yourself? If not, then where is your mind?

Are you thinking about to-do lists? Are you resenting what you have to do? Are you trying to get this over and done so that you can move on to the next thing?

What reality are you creating in this moment?

How are you engaging with life in this moment?

How is this reality making you feel?

Are you at peace and happy?

What part of your story is preventing you from being at peace and happy? Do you need to keep telling that story?

Imagine letting it go. Stop telling the story and come back to the present. Look around you and see where you are. See who you're with. Experience what you're doing. Be present.

Becoming aware of the miracles of life

You can begin with a breathing and centering exercise. Turn back inward, reconnecting with self.

Open beyond your stories, opinions, and judgments. Open to experience in open-minded awareness.

Imagine yourself in a place where you go frequently. This should be a pleasant place but nothing out of the ordinary. Imagine yourself sitting quietly in this place, giving yourself the time and space to really engage with it.

Look around you and notice all of the miraculous things you see. See the beauty of the shapes and colors. See the life unfolding before your eyes. See the work that went into creating whatever it is that you are seeing, whether it be by man or nature. Feel a deep sense of gratitude for whatever it is you are seeing.

Now do the same for what you are smelling. Smell the forest

floor, or the fresh breeze, or the coffee roasting. Smell the depth of life in your surroundings and feel a deep sense of gratitude.

Now turn to your sense of hearing and listen for all the miraculous sounds of life. Listen in gratitude to the water trickling, or the bird singing, or your dog snoring. Listen and feel the joy of being able to hear life.

Now turn to your sense of touch and notice all the sensations associated with where you are. Look at each sensation as a reminder of the miraculous gift of life. Feel grateful for the ability to feel.

Notice that these little miracles are always around you, you just have to pay attention to get in touch with the joy they bring.

These changes will not occur overnight. The practices will need consistent attention for a permanent shift to occur. Our thought patterns have been running free for a very long time, so creating new pathways will take some time. It's like when you start taking a new path through the woods. At first it is a struggle to break through the brush and trees. You have to find the best route to follow and spend a lot of energy cutting vegetation and clearing rocks. But each time you walk the path, it becomes clearer and easier to find. Eventually, you will have traveled it so many times that you could walk it with your eyes closed. This is how we form new pathways within the brain. At first it takes much effort and we have to pay close attention to what we are thinking and how we are reacting. But as we continue to stay present and notice our thoughts, it becomes easier and easier, until one day it happens naturally.

4

Mindful of Our Emotions

Our emotions play a big part in who we are and how we see the world. They are also what make us spiritual beings, able to engage with life by feeling it pulse through us in an energetic flow. Emotions interact with our entire being, playing out in the mind and throughout our entire body. They tell us a lot about our environment and establish our relationship to it, altering how we participate in the world. Emotions are a great gift to us and should be treated with much respect and kindness. With the right amount of nurturing, they can help us reach our full spiritual potential.

Emotions carry much wisdom because they evolved through time to keep us safe and thriving. [32] If engaged with functionally, they can inform us of dangers and life giving opportunities. If engaged with negatively, they can enslave us in debilitating mental states. Most mental illnesses are caused by emotional disorders.[32] Healing our emotions can heal our mind and body.

In order for emotions to enhance rather than hinder us, we have to understand them and how they affect the way we see and interact with life. This is also known as emotional intelligence or the ability to recognize and understand emotions in yourself and others, and your ability to use this awareness to manage your behavior and relationships.[6] Daniel Goleman describes four different domains of emotional intelligence. The first is self-awareness, or the ability to know what we are feeling and why. It is our moral compass. The second is self-management, or our ability to handle distressing emotions in a productive way. The third is empathy, or the ability to understand others' emotions. And the fourth is the ability to apply all three together to form skilled relationships.[21] We must develop all four skills in order for our emotions to become a useful and integrated part of our lives.

When we manage our emotions well, we reduce stress and anxiety, heighten self-confidence, increase compassion, and improve attention and concentration.[16; 33; 28; 38; 44; 24; 18; 25] We also increase our ability to hear different opinions and be in contact with novel situations, allowing us to learn and grow. We can be fully present for and receptive to incoming information. Sitting with the input without reacting immediately allows for better integration of impressions we are receiving.[26] When we speak, we do so meaningfully, having taken the time to fully process the situation and our emotions before responding.[16; 26] This allows us to be more present and compassionate within our relationships.

The only danger in having emotions lies in suppressing them

and leaving them unattended. They then fester, mold within us, and explode in very harmful ways. Some signs of emotions that are out of control are abuse, inter-group wars, hatred, and discrimination.[21] We all know that these signs are far too prevalent in our world today. This is because we have been programmed to leave our emotions unaddressed. We are told schools are not the place for them, the workplace is not the place for them, public spaces are not the place for them; this leaves us only about fifteen percent of our day when we are allowed to be emotional. The problem with this is that our emotions are present one hundred percent of the day because we are emotional beings, and when we suppress or deny emotions, we cause ourselves harm.

When addressed and nurtured, emotions are the spice of life, transforming the mundane into a meaningful and personal adventure. In order to use them to enhance our lives, we must first become aware of them. This means that we have to become comfortable with feeling our emotions and then sitting with them long enough to understand them. If we have many unaddressed traumas, then this process may be quite difficult, and we will want to start slowly. If this is the case for you, then stay with these first two exercises for as long as you need to before diving into the deeper topics.

You can use the following exercises to become aware of your emotions.

2.4.1 EXERCISES ON BECOMING AWARE OF EMOTIONS

Identifying emotions

You can begin with a breathing exercise and then step into that open space behind thought.

As you begin to observe your thoughts, begin to notice if there are emotions associated with the thoughts. Name the emotion that you find.

Now switch your attention to your body and begin to feel all the ways in which this emotion manifests within your body.

Where do you tighten?

Where does your energy go?

What hurts?

Do any muscles weaken?

What is your posture?

What is your heart feeling?

What are your hands doing?

What is your facial expression?

Now come back to the mind and notice how this emotion is affecting your thoughts.

What are you thinking about yourself?

What are you thinking about the other and the world?

What perspective do you have about the world?

Is this the only true perspective?

How do you interact with the world when you are having this emotion?

Who are you being?

You can continue this exercise by scanning through your day and noticing other times during the day that this emotion was present. Notice how it changed who you were being.

You can also use this meditation throughout the day, becoming aware of when this emotion is present and catching it in the moment. Do this exercise many times to become aware of all the different emotions present within you. You will be surprised to realize that they are always present and they are always affecting who you are being.

Transitioning away from strong emotions

As you begin to do the previous exercise more often, you may come in contact with strong emotions that are too difficult to sit with.

It may feel like they are suffocating you or turning your whole world dark. In this situation, you will need to switch your attention back to present moment awareness.

Tune into your senses and begin to name five things that you see around you. Then close your eyes and name four things you hear, then three things you smell, and two physical sensations that you feel. Stay with your breath and your present moment experience until your emotion softens and you are able to continue with the practice.

Once we recognize all of the emotions that are constantly at play in our lives, we can begin to allow their presence and observe them. This observation then leads to a deeper understanding. In order to sit with our emotions, we have to find some stable grounding so that we don't get swept away or drowned by them. We find this grounding in our breath and in our present moment awareness. The breath reminds us that we have the tools to handle what we feel and that we are safe in the present moment. It is best to do this work in a calm environment where you have the time and space to be still and relaxed before and after the practice.

When we feel like we have a sturdy base, we can invite our emotions in. This is where we combat all of those stories we've been told about not allowing our emotions in, to buck up and turn away from what we feel. Soften all of those words in your head and create an inviting place in your mind and heart where you welcome the emotion and allow it to be felt. Feelings need to be consistently cycled through, coming to the surface, being addressed, and then returning to their seed within us. When they are allowed to surface and experience the sun and fresh air, they soften and return to a calm state. If we hold them down and never let them cycle through, they turn darker and scarier, becoming more and more of a threat to us. They start to seem larger than life and it becomes more difficult to allow them to surface because we are afraid they may explode. This is why you must invite them up frequently. Invite them to have tea with you. Look them in the eyes and tell them that they are welcome. They too are a part of you. They too belong.

In order to be comfortable feeling, we have to notice how and why we resist our emotions. Past experiences or societal teachings may have led us to believe that feeling emotions leads to negative outcomes. We may have seen emotional outbursts that cause chain reactions of destruction to self and others. Emotions are only destructive when they are left unattended for too long and then get so unmanageable that they release in explosive ways. This is not the true nature of emotions. We can relearn how to relate to our emotions by understanding our false beliefs around what feeling them will do to us. Look into your beliefs about how each emotion expresses itself and who you become when feeling them. You may find that you don't have to respond in a negative way to emotions. You can still feel them without becoming someone you don't want to be or harming the world around you. You can reprogram how you relate to and express your emotions so that experiencing them no longer has a negative impact on your life.

Once we no longer see our emotions as our enemies here to disrupt our lives, we can open up to experiencing them and listening to them. I like to think about it like inviting my emotions to have tea with me. When you invite a friend to have tea you have no agenda, you are not trying to make them go away or change them, you simply want to be in their presence and learn how they are doing. The same is true for inviting our emotions into our awareness. We don't approach them with the intent to change them, push them away, tell them they're wrong, or fix them. We simply want to be in their presence and learn what they are telling us about our own experience. This interaction with our emotions is done in a safe environment where we can be calm and quiet and we hold our emotions within our heart space. The space within us that is free of judgment and accepts all experiences with love, compassion, and peace.

You can use the following exercise to invite your emotions up into your heart.

2.4.2 EXERCISE ON INVITING YOUR EMOTIONS INTO YOUR HEART SPACE

Noticing your relationship to emotion

You can begin with a breathing exercise and then follow your breath into your heart space.

Recall a time when you began to feel an emotion but forced it away. Examine your reaction to that emotion.

Why did you react the way you did?

What were you afraid of?

What do you think feeling that emotion will do to you?

What will feeling result in?

How has that emotion manifested in your words and your actions in the past?

Does it have to manifest that way?

Notice your relationship to that emotion.

Has feeling that emotion led to undesired outcomes before?

What were those outcomes?

Did the emotion have to lead to them?

Imagine yourself feeling that emotion in a healthy grounded state. How do you react?

What do you say and do?

Imagine yourself remaining calm and peaceful even in the presence of that emotion. Notice what relationship you have to that emotion now. Now are you afraid of that emotion?

Inviting your emotions for tea

You can begin with a breathing exercise and then follow your breath into your heart space.

Feel the true nature of your heart space. It is open, loving, compassionate, and kind. In the heart space, there is room for all things. All things belong, even difficult emotions.

Recognize how this heart space is rooted in the foundation of your being and then when connected with these roots you are grounded enough to handle all things.

Allow your heart space to grow wider and wider opening in non-judgmental awareness.

Imagine inviting your emotion into this space that the heart has created. It's warm and cozy and all things can be held here.

Tell your emotion that it is welcome, that it too belongs, and that you would like to be with it and experience it.

This is like inviting a dear friend to tea. You really want to be present with them, to look them in the eyes and hear what they have to say. Invite your emotion to have tea with you.

Use the strength of the heart space and all of its love and compassion to feel safe here with your emotion. Remember all of your resources to take care of self and nurture self and use that awareness to feel safe here with your emotion.

You may even imagine the heart space and all of your self-care techniques as a kind and caring companion who can be present for the suffering part of you. Allow this strong and stable side of you to give you the courage to be vulnerable with this emotion.

Once we are able to sit with our emotions, we begin to explore their true nature. We notice their impermanence, which reduces their negative effects and increases emotional intelligence.[14; 33; 38] It does this by reducing our reactivity and enabling us to manage our perspective.[3] Instead of being swept away on a current of emotion, we remain present with them, feel them, understand them, and then allow them to move on. We enter into a peaceful and organic relationship with emotion.

The actual physiological effects of an emotion caused by a chemical process in the body only last for ninety seconds.[40] After that time, it is our own thoughts and stories that are prolonging the emotional response. We replay the story and re-project the blame over and over, regenerating the emotion within us. When those initial ninety seconds have passed, the only thing causing the emotion is us. If we could simply recognize an emotion, feel it, and then bring our focus back to the present, we wouldn't get trapped in negative emotional states.

The real cause of emotions is not necessarily some immediately present stimuli, but instead the interaction of these with a causal history stored in memory.[32] We may have been feeding our emotion story long before a triggering event happened, which is why the event was able to trigger us in the first place. The external events that we were experiencing interact with the story we had been telling ourselves and produce the emotional response that we ourselves assigned to the event. Without our interpretation of the event linked to previous memories, there would be no emotional response.

I always use the example of when I would get angry at a student when teaching. The actual trigger could only produce anger because of the stories I was telling myself before the event would happen. First of all, I had the underlying expectation of how students should behave in class. Then, the evening before the triggering event, I may tell myself how this one kid always starts a conversation right in the middle of a lecture and how rude that is. I then tell myself that he better not do it tomorrow. As I'm getting ready for work the next day, I replay the past behavior of the kid and remind myself of how irritating it is. As the kids enter the class, I remind myself again as I set expectations that he better not do it today. Then, during the lecture, he starts a conversation and I choose to light my flame of anger. Essentially, I had created my own anger.

I could have pacified my anger at any one of these points along the build up process. I could have chosen to have different expectations. I could have told myself a different story, looking into what that child's needs may have been rather than focusing on what he was doing wrong. I could have interacted with him differently when he entered the room instead of feeding my story about why he is irritating. I could have taken a pause after he triggered me to notice my feelings before reacting in anger.

Most of the time, we have the choice of how we experience our emotions and we choose to feed them by the stories we tell.

Sometimes these memories and stories are unconscious, which makes them harder to understand. In the case of PTSD or anxiety disorders, we have subconscious memories that are triggered by stimuli that resemble the environment or conditions of past experiences. We then react emotionally to a stored fear memory rather than our current situation. Sometimes the trigger of these fear responses may be the state of our body. If we have experienced an elevated heart rate during severe trauma, then when our heart rate goes up under ordinary circumstances, it may trigger a panic attack.[32] This makes it difficult for us to explain why we feel certain emotions and react the way we do because they are generated by programmed reactions that we aren't aware of.

The more space we can give ourselves between when we feel an emotion and when we respond, the more able we are to understand the origin of the emotion and generate an appropriate response. When we are in an unconscious reactive state, our limbic system feeds information directly from the thalamus to the amygdala, skips the cortex where higher processing can be used to determine the gravity and intensity of a situation, and causes us to experience explosive emotions.[32] Mindfulness gives us the ability to process information in the prefrontal cortex and become fully aware of what is happening before responding.[36] By simply naming an emotion and becoming aware of it, we free ourselves from the limbic system, coming away from fight, flight, freeze into positive response.[5]

Understanding the nature of our emotions decreases our fear

of them. When we see that they are impermanent, we no longer feel the need to control them or push them away because we understand that they are constantly coming and going on their own. When we understand that emotions are generated by our own memories and stories, we don't put so much pressure on the world around us to maintain our positive state. We begin to trust our own ability to generate positive emotions regardless of what external conditions exist. We recognize that our emotions don't necessarily reflect our current situation and that by stepping into present moment awareness, we can soften their effects. All of these insights offer us a much more peaceful relationship with our emotional experiences.

We can begin by exploring our emotional triggers. This could be a physical state of the body that reminds us of a previous emotional experience putting us back into it. The trigger could also be something in our environment that reminds us of a previous emotional experience or indicates that one of our basic needs is under threat. It may also be an event or something someone does that confirms a story we've been telling about what needs we were expecting to be met that weren't. Notice the expectations you had for the world and the people around you. Were they realistic?

These triggers are what initiate the emotional response within us. Once they are triggered, it is up to us whether or not they continue to be fed and what reaction they will generate. If we dive into the story of the emotion and justify its presence with blame then we become the victim of the situation and of our emotion usually generating a negative reaction. It is helpful to come out of the story of the emotion and re-engage with our current reality. Check in with yourself and make sure that you are in a safe environment and that you are capable of meeting all of your basic needs. If this is the case, then you can begin to explore the intensity of the emotion and if it is really fitting to the situation. Does your current situation really deserve this emotional reaction? What would happen if you were to calm down? Are you really okay? If so, then take a few deep breaths and re-engage with the situation in full conscious awareness rather than from an emotional state. This will allow you to generate an appropriate response that is beneficial to you and the people around you.

You can begin to observe the nature of your emotions with the following exercises.

2.4.3 EXERCISES ON OBSERVING THE NATURE OF EMOTIONS

Recognizing the story behind your emotion

You can begin with the previous exercise on naming your emotion and then inviting it to tea.

Once your emotion is present within your heart space being held and supported, you can begin to investigate the story behind it. You may want to start with the body becoming curious if the trigger of the emotion was in fact a physical sensation within the body.

Was your heart rate elevated?

Was your breathing constricted?

Was your blood pressure elevated?

Coming back to the breath and present moment awareness can help these physiological symptoms to calm.

Now, bring your attention up into the mind. Notice what story you are telling that is keeping the emotion alive within you.

Are you placing blame?

Are you desperately needing something to be different or fixed?

Are you resisting something or clinging to something?

What perspective do you have of self, the other, and the world?

Is this true?

Are you reacting to your current experience or out of its resemblance to a previous experience?

Is your current situation really deserving of this reaction?

Now, look around you. Come back to the present moment. Silence the story.

What's really happening?

Are you safe?

Are you okay?

Is there any immediate threat?

Do you need to remain in this emotional state?

Settle back into your breath and the present moment, allowing the emotion to soften. You may want to repeat to yourself that in this moment, you are okay and safe.

Listening to what the emotion is really telling you

This exercise can be done after the previous one. Once you have allowed your emotion to be present and then soften, you can begin to investigate what the emotion was trying to tell you. Normally our emotions are trying to keep us safe or alert us to important life-providing opportunities.

What was it that made you unsettled?

Was it alerting you to a potential danger?

Does this danger really exist or was it just a perceived potential danger triggered by a certain environmental condition that you have associated with danger in the past?

Was it alerting you to a potential opportunity?

These are feelings of excitement, love, or desire.

What were you feeling these emotions for?

Is this thing really that urgent?

Do you need to react right away?

Is your reaction actually going to attract them?

Was this emotion pointing to an unmet need?

Maybe the need to be heard, accepted, loved, or valued, or maybe the need for safety and shelter. Is this really an urgent unmet need?

Now that you understand why the emotion arose, it shouldn't have the same urgency. Allow the emotion to soften as you settle into the understanding of your actual situation. Notice the reaction that you usually have to the emotion.

Does this reaction get you closer to what you were really wanting?

Does the reaction help or harm you?

What response would actually move you closer to your desired outcome? Imagine yourself responding in this way. How does it feel?

What response do you get from the world and the others?

Did it move you closer to who you want to be and the outcome you wanted to experience?

Once we have recognized our emotion, allowed it to be present, and understood its nature, we can nurture it. This is a very important step because it is what helps regulate the emotion and allows us to detach from negative thought patterns.[25; 2] Our ability to regulate our inner state has been proven to improve our behavior and relationships.[24] We do not want our neocortical cognition to dominate our emotional systems meaning that we use logic and reasoning to avoid feeling. We just want a harmonious integration of reason and passion that will allow us to better know our true feelings and use them more effectively in daily life.[32]

The nurturing stage is what allows us to choose healthy thought patterns so that emotions can better serve us. By meeting the needs of our emotions and reassuring ourselves that they are not going to lead to our death or destruction, we are open to using them to enhance our lives.

We start by understanding the true needs of the emotion and then nurturing those hurt places. This step is linked to our spiritual well-being because often a trust in something bigger than ourselves helps ease these hard to meet needs. When we look deeply into the cause of our emotions, oftentimes we find the basic human needs for love, safety, acceptance, and belonging. When we experience negative emotions they are pointing out the danger of these needs not being met. When we experience positive emotions they motivate us to pursue the present possibility of these needs to be met. The suffering in life is generated by the impossibility for these needs to be met at all moments. Humans will disappoint us: based on their own traumas, they may not be able to give us true unconditional love and acceptance. Because life is always changing and unstable, we may not always be safe and have a place where we belong. So, what do we do with this dilemma? We become comfortable with our needs not being met by worldly situations and beings and turn to something greater for our comfort.

When you begin to offer your emotions the nurturing they need, you will not look to external sources. You will be finding the sources inward, in your own heart, and your own practice. This is because external conditions are uncertain, unpredictable, and inconsistent. Only our internal sources can provide us unconditional constant love and care. These internal comforts may range from your spiritual practice to your own self-love and grounding. They may be the realization that you are connected to all things embraced and held within the entire system. They may be your belief in a higher power or God who provides you with everything you truly need. The key is that you know you have the ability to access these sources no matter what is going on in the world around you.

You can use the following exercise to nurture your emotions.

2.4.4 EXERCISE ON NURTURING YOUR EMOTIONS

Nurture your emotions

You can begin with the exercise of listening to your emotion's true needs. Arrive at the root cause of the emotion.

Was it a cry for safety, love, acceptance, or belonging?

Examine where you were looking to meet this need.

Was this a consistent and unconditional source of this need?

If it was a condition of the world or a person?

These are not consistent providers of all of our needs. Accept the flaws of the source of this need. Humans are flawed and cannot always give unconditional support and love. The world is flawed and cannot always be a place of safety and love.

Forgive them for this.

Now go inward. Enter your own heart space. Connect with that truth within you. Recognize how you are connected to all things.

Know that this source of love and safety and belonging resides within you.

Know that when we accept ourselves, we always belong. When we love ourselves, we are always loved. When we accept our place in the greater system, we always find safety within it.

Find your source of these needs. You can say this out loud or to yourself, "I am here for you. You are loved. You are accepted just as you are. You are safe. Everything belongs within the greater system."

Offer yourself anything else that your emotion is asking for. Rest in this place of peace and acceptance.

Once our needs are met and our emotion has pacified, we can once again participate in the world intentionally. When our emotions are out of control and neglected, we show up as tainted versions of ourselves, demanding more of the world than it is able to give. But when our emotions have been expressed and nurtured, we can appreciate the world for what it is able to give and offer the best of ourselves in return.

Consistent and reliable sources of nurturing allow us to show up in the world as the best version of ourselves. Each one of our responses will lead to a better understanding of self and of the world around us. With each emotional experience, we will develop deeper connections to self and others. When we are no longer dependent on others for our emotional needs, we free ourselves from the disappointments that lead to destructive reactions. We can be present for others without the fear of being triggered into a version of ourselves that we aren't proud of.

You can use the following exercise to connect with this nurtured version of yourself, offering the world the best of you.

2.4.5 EXERCISE ON OFFERING THE WORLD THE BEST OF YOU

Offering the world the best of you

After having completed the work with your emotions, observe who you are being in this settled and grounded state.

How does your body feel?

What are your energy levels?

What is your posture?

What is your facial expression?

What are you telling yourself about the world, other people, and yourself? Who are you being?

When you are fully nurtured, what are you expecting from the world and others?

What are you receiving from the world and your loved ones?

What is your relationship to the world and your friends and family?

What are you offering the world and humankind and how are they receiving it?

What is your purpose?

Feel this best version of yourself in your heart and core.

Know that being this person is always a possibility if you consistently nurture yourself and look to the right sources for all your fundamental needs.

Our emotions are a reflection of our relationship to self and the world. If they are consistently negative, then we are choosing to tell ourselves negative stories about the world and our place in it. When we nurture ourselves and focus on all the sources of love, acceptance, belonging, safety, and nourishment within and around us, then we no longer dwell in negative emotions. We can feel each emotion without fear, learn from it, nurture its needs, and move through it.

5

Mindful of Our Spirit

We cannot heal completely without healing our spirit. Our spirit gives meaning and vibrancy to our lives by connecting our being with the rest of the cosmos. The spirit is what allows us to survive suffering by finding something greater than ourselves to rely on and find purpose in. Without the spirit, life is a self-absorbed process of avoiding suffering and clinging to pleasure. It is spirit that leads to self-transcendence and a reaching outward in compassion and generosity towards others. As Victor Frankl says, this reaching outward is what being human is all about: "It is being always directed and pointing to something or someone other than oneself, to a meaning to fulfill or another human being to encounter, a cause to serve or a person to love." [19]

In order to heal our spirit, we must find a spiritual practice that speaks the true language of our heart. Our heart's spirituality does not require a set of beliefs or dogma. It exists in the way we live and interact in the world, not in the views we believe in or the rules we follow. As Eckhart Tolle says, "Having a belief system-a set of thoughts that you regard as the absolute truth-does not make you spiritual no matter what the nature of those beliefs is. The new spirituality, the transformation of consciousness, means letting go of identification with form, dogma, and rigid belief systems and discovering the original depth that is hidden within your own spiritual tradition at the same time as within yourself. Spiritual has everything to do with your state of consciousness and in turn determines how you act in the world and interact with others." [43]

The first step to finding our heart's spirituality is to let go of the need to know or prove our own truth. Every individual will have a unique relationship to the spirit of the world, and in order to encourage spiritual growth, we must allow spiritual freedom. In order to touch the greater wisdom within and around us, we must first be free of our own narrow minded opinions and admit that we don't know. Spirituality is constantly evolving and changing. It needs to remain fluid and a bit mysterious. It is in the seeking not in the knowing that we touch spiritual wisdom.

We already did some of this work when we examined the nature of mind, but now we need to direct this openness to our spirit. For many of us, this goes against the deep rooted teachings of our religions. We may have been asked not to question, not to search for ourselves, but to trust in dogma, ritual, and tradition. This mindset has prevented us from connecting with the spirituality that resides within our heart, and we must break free of these chains. We should question and we should search. We should dig deep into the heart of our own practice so that we can better understand others. As Thich Nhat Hanh says, "By understanding your own tradition better, you also develop increased respect, consideration, and understanding for others."[22]

This does not mean that we have to leave our religion or tradition behind, it just means that we need to understand it at a much deeper level and open ourselves to the possibility that other traditions may help us in the process. We cannot be afraid of different beliefs; they are what help us to understand our own even better.

I grew up in a Christian family. My mom encouraged our whole family to attend church each Sunday by offering post service donuts. I never felt very enthusiastic about Christianity, and as time went on, my lack of enthusiasm turned into a full on hate. I would watch as good Christian families went to church on Sunday and then returned home to drink themselves into a stupor or abuse their wives and children. Religion did not seem to be helping people heal—in fact, quite the opposite. The guilt and shame associated with it seemed to be keeping people from admitting the truth to themselves and others, which was preventing everybody from healing. As my own family fell apart due to emotional abuse and addiction, I began to hate Christianity even more. It felt like a big dark lie that everyone was telling to avoid the personal responsibility associated with truth.

For many years, I avoided any form of spirituality, associating it with lies and manipulation. But as my own internal pain started growing and every other vice I had was either exposed or unavailable, I knew the healing had to come from something bigger than me. So I began a different kind of spiritual journey.

My introduction back into the spirit began with a book by Thich Nhat Hanh given to me by a counselor, *Reconciliation: Healing Your Inner Child*. Thich Nhat Hanh explained mindfulness so simply, with no bells and whistles, no guilt, no ritual, no dogma, no rules, just truth—a truth that rang so deep it felt like my own lost soul speaking to me after a long silence. This book opened the door to mindfulness which opened the door to Buddhism.

This is when I began to study meditation and Buddhist philosophy at the Shedrub Choekhor Ling Monastery outside of Geneva, Switzerland. Because Buddhism was more of a philosophy than a religion, I felt safe within its teachings. It used logic and wisdom to explain the human experience and a way out of suffering. I was encouraged to ask questions, to search, to experience for myself how the practices worked. The perspectives and practices were changing the way I saw myself, others, and the world and for the first time since my early childhood, I was starting to feel tiny moments of inner peace. So I kept going. I did five different retreats at Thich Nhat Hanh's center Plum Village in France, two different teacher trainings at his center in Paris, and I worked with a Sangha in Geneva. I did my master's research on the use of meditation and mindfulness in language acquisition, and studied how the practice altered and healed the brain. I did a ten day silent meditation retreat through the Vipassana Center in Switzerland, and by the end of all of this, I was convinced that Buddhism was my home.

I then returned to Colorado and wanted to explore Tibetan Buddhism further. I completed a three month study internship at the Tara Mandala Practice Center in Pagosa Springs, Colorado. What I found here humbled my confidence in Buddhism and reminded me that no religion or practice is free of the human condition. At this center, I found ritual, power struggles, fear, manipulation, and lies preventing people from seeing their personal responsibility in the experiences they were having.

This experience with Buddhism freed me from the feeling that I had found the right way when Christianity had been the wrong way. It reminded me that all belief systems have their weaknesses and that it is up to us to relate to the teachings in ways that help rather than harm. It brought me back to the teachings of Thich Nhat Hanh, who tells us that by studying other belief systems we can deepen our understanding of our own and heal our relationship to it. This experience healed my relationship to Christianity. I still do not practice Christianity, but I no longer hate it. I can read the Bible and Christian teachings and find many great insights that point to truth without getting caught in the dogma.

I now approach spirituality as an ever-evolving relationship to the world. As my understanding of self changes, so does my understanding of my place in the world and the energy that connects us all. I don't assume that I have all the answers or that I ever will. The curious exploration of an open heart keeps the spirit alive in all of us.

You can use the following exercises to help you to open to different beliefs and perspectives.

2.5.1 EXERCISES ON OPENING TO SPIRITUAL DIFFERENCE

Noticing my clinging to belief

You can begin with a breathing exercise and then open the mind. Once you have become the observer rather than the thinker, you can begin to examine the beliefs that you cling to.

When did you first hear that these beliefs were so important?

What did they do for you?

What are they doing for you now?

Notice how your need for these beliefs to be right affects who you are.

What does protecting these do to your interaction with others who have different views?

What does protecting these beliefs do to your ability to love and accept everyone?

Who do you become when you try to prove your beliefs?

Is this who you want to be? Is this a true representation of your spiritual self?

Now, repeat to yourself, "I don't know. I don't need to know. Something so much greater than me is holding all of this."

Rest in the comfort and ease of not having to know.

Feel the peace that it brings you.

Notice who you are able to be when you are not clinging to your belief or needing to prove it to others.

Are you softer?

Are you more loving?

Are you better able to live out your spirituality?

Opening to difference

This exercise should be done after the previous one. Once you have noticed the beliefs that you cling to, picture yourself holding them on a piece of paper right in front of your face.

Notice how when you hold them this close to you, they become all you can see. You cannot see anything else when all you want to look at is your own beliefs.

Now, begin to distance yourself from these beliefs. Take them out from in front of your face and look around. See the world around you.

Notice what other people see.

Notice how other people think.

Explore the varying beliefs of the world. Discover new cultures and what they believe. Experience different religions to understand what they believe. See the beauty that exists within them.

They are not right or wrong. You are not right or wrong. Hold your belief lightly in the palm of your hand as you explore the world around you. Give the belief the freedom to change and transform or fly away.

Notice how beautiful it becomes when it is given the freedom to evolve.

Notice how it interacts with the world and adapts to wherever it goes.

Now, when it comes back to you and you choose to hold it again, it will be in its genuine form and you will not feel the need to cling so tightly to it.

Once we find peace and acceptance in not knowing, we can begin to explore what the true nature of our heart's spirituality is. This will look different for everyone. You do not have to relate to spirituality in the same way as anyone else. A spirituality of the heart comes from the essence of what your practice is and how you live it out. It is who you want to be in the world and the energies you want to share with others. As Thich Nhat Hanh says, we represent our spiritual tradition "just by the way we walk, sit, and smile."[22] Our spiritual practice is who we are.

In order to find your heart's spirituality, you must know yourself. As the contender in the Gospel of Thomas says, "whoever has not known himself has known nothing but whoever has known himself has simultaneously achieved knowledge about the depth of all things."[35]

This work will continue through time with consistent contemplative practices, and every day your knowledge of self will continue to evolve and deepen, revealing more and more of your true nature. This process requires you to devote yourself to wisdom and to accept the unexpected places that it leads you. Deepak Chopra describes wisdom by saying it "connects you to who you really are, as you discover and then use what is unique to you. Wisdom is a surprise, it defies expectations, it leads to an unpredictable place. It is elusive and changeable. It cannot be taught. It is contrary to reason and sense and social practicalities.[9] There is no certainty when we devote ourselves to this form of wisdom.

As we come closer to understanding our own true nature, we touch the nature of the divine. Dialogue One of Mary Magdalene speaks to this, saying "The son of humanity already exists within you...and those who seek him there will find him."[41] Einstein touched on the same knowledge saying "Whatever there is of God in the universe, it must work itself out and express itself through us."[15]

In order to touch our true nature, we have to arrive at the very epicenter of our being, free of all the worldly cravings, attachments, traumas, programming, and ignorance. We have to go to what lies beneath all of our own blind spots and see the essence of who we are. Thomas Merton explains this well in his essay *A Member of the Human Race*. "At the center of our being is a point of nothingness which is untouched by sin and illusion, a point of pure truth which belongs entirely to God and remains inaccessible to the fantasies of our own mind or the brutalities of our own will."[34] God, or pure heart, is simply love, compassion, peace, and acceptance. All else are humanly needs and desires that trap us in our own illusions.

So the process of finding our true spirituality has to begin with a true understanding of self. As we dive deeper into our own inner-workings, we find the wisdom of the heart. And in this wisdom that resides at the core of our being, we find God.

You can use the following exercises to begin to touch your heart's true nature. You can come back to this practice over and over, each time finding new wisdom and a deeper understanding of your heart's wisdom.

2.5.2 EXERCISE ON CONNECTING WITH YOUR HEART'S TRUE NATURE

Listening to the heart

This exercise is best done after completing the exercises 2.5.1 so that you are able to see past the limitations of imposed beliefs. Once you are open and present, focus your attention inward focusing on your heart center.

Feel the heart expanding and contracting with each breath. Allow the heart to open to the world on the inhalation and then re-center on your heart's values on the exhalation. Open at the same time as centering on the heart's truth. You can begin to listen to the heart.

What does the heart value most?

How does the heart want to interact with the world?

What does the heart want to offer the world?

What really matters to the heart?

How does the heart see you, the world, and others?

Who are you being when you are living from the heart?

Where does your grounding and foundation come from?

What does it feel like to live from the heart?

Sit in this feeling and observe how it feels to be in the world when grounded in the heart. See who you are being. See what you are offering. Observe what you say and how others receive your words.

See yourself living from the heart.

When we are living from the heart, we begin to see the true nature of God, the world, and our place within it. We see the interworking of life and the undeniable truth that there is a greater force or energy pulsing through it all. As Albert Einstein says, "Try and penetrate with our limited means the secrets of nature, and you will find that behind all the discernible layers and connections, there remains something subtle, intangible, and inexplicable. Veneration for this force beyond anything we can comprehend is my religion."[15]

How we identify and connect with this force may be unique to us, or it may align with a faith, practice, or religion. It does not matter how you get in touch with it as long as you can relate to it on a personal level. This personal relationship is what will help you see that "there is no separation between a creator and that which is created. As the self is realized, the divinity of all creation in all its expressions goes forth with shining power and absoluteness. It is complete and total unity and oneness."[23]

When we act and live in unison with this greater force, we begin to walk, speak, breathe, and live our spiritual reality. We begin to see that "God is pure consciousness, the essence of who you are. God is a process, it builds upon itself. You will know that you are on the right path because every step brings insight, clarity, and expanded experiences."[9] This is when we can truly use every experience as an opportunity to wake up to spirituality to grow and transform with every step forward.

You can use the following exercises to help you get in touch with this greater force in and around you. Each time you do this practice you will deepen your integration into the greater system.

2.5.3 EXERCISES ON CONNECTING WITH THAT WHICH IS GREATER

Moving beyond the self

You can begin with a body scan. As you scan the body, feeling all the sensations in each part of the body, recognize the sensation of energy that exists equally throughout the body. You can feel it flowing from one part to the next. This subtle vibration that lets you know that you are alive.

Focus all of your attention on this vibration. Feel it in every cell of your body. As you are feeling it, expand your awareness outward. Grow your field of awareness wider and wider. Stay with the awareness of this vibration of life force.

Notice how this force expands beyond you, beyond your body and being.

Feel how it also exists in the air around you, in the objects around you, and in the trees, plants, and animals. Notice how it flows through all living beings.

Notice how it is also present in what we consider to be non-living beings.

As you identify more with this greater energy and less with the boundaries of self, you will begin to feel this flow between you and the external world.

Feel how you can float on this energy in a harmonious process of giving and receiving.

Feel how you are held within this greater energy, supported, and nurtured. Trust that all things belong here within the greater system.

Relaxing into the flow of that which is greater

Begin by expanding beyond self. Feel the energy within and around you. Notice the ways in which you try to control, manipulate, and push the world to meet your needs.

Notice what this does to your relationship with this greater energy.

Are you able to trust?

Are you able to see where the world is leading you?

Are you able to see the abundance around you?

Are you able to see the resources available to you?

How does the world react when you fight and push for your own agenda? Are you tired?

Now begin to soften.

Let go of your need to know and control.

Trust that you are held within this greater system.

Trust that this greater force will carry you where you need to go.

Trust that everything you experience is held within the greater system that it belongs and is giving you exactly what you need.

Surrender your own needs and desires to those of the greater system.

Listen and observe for where you are meant to go and what you are meant to do.

Act within the greater system from the energies of your heart.

Find a harmonious collaboration between your inner ideas and aspirations and the ones the greater system has for you. They will come together and lead you to your true purpose.

Now that we are working in unison with that which is greater, we can begin to live our true purpose. Living with purpose is what gives us a reason to participate in the world. This doesn't have to be linked to our job or role in society. It shows up more in who we are being in whatever we are doing.

A spiritual purpose is one that is generated from a direct connection with that which is greater. David Hawkins describes spiritual work as a selfless service and surrender to the will of God.[23] Our attention shifts from being self-serving to being other-serving. We rise above self and use what is unique to us in ways that can serve the greater good.

My own spiritual journey led me to a job title that reflects my purpose, but this does not always have to be the case. Through the first few years of my spiritual journey, I never once thought that I would eventually teach mindfulness to others. My intentions were always to heal myself so that I could show up better for others. The more I healed, the more I realized that mindfulness was becoming who I was and that it is what I have to offer the world.

I always had a heart for helping others, and for the first eleven years of my working life that had shown up as being a teacher. Teaching is a profession that I greatly admire. Those who dedicate their lives to encourage the mental, emotional, and social growth of others are saints in my mind. However, once I returned from my deep dive into mindfulness and meditation, I returned to teaching and felt like something was missing. I tried to teach mindfulness in the schools and designed a whole curriculum around brain science and mindfulness, but it still wasn't enough. I didn't want to bring a small dose of mindfulness into the schools, I wanted to fully immerse myself in the practice and dedicate my life to it. So I quit teaching and started my own business as a mindfulness coach, which at the time was an unheard of profession. I had some people in my life telling me that it was inspiring to pursue my own passion and others, including my father, who thought I was crazy for leaving a decent job with good benefits. But once you discover your heart's purpose and you set out to live it, each step fuels your soul and grows your connection to the greater life source filling you with an unstoppable energy. I certainly had many, many moments of doubt, failure, exhaustion, and sadness, but they were always outweighed by the motivation that came from something so much greater than me.

On your healing journey, you will uncover your own deepest passions and loves and they will fuel your purpose. They do not have to turn into your career, but they will allow you to share your true self with the world.

2.5.4 EXERCISES ON FINDING YOUR PURPOSE

Identifying your unique purpose

You can begin with a breathing exercise and coming back home to self.

Connect with your body, becoming aware of every part of you. Notice the things that your body does really well. Notice how it takes care of you. Notice how it allows you to participate in the world.

You can also notice its limitations and what these teach you. How these limitations help you to have compassion for others. How they've helped you to grow. Listen to your body and the energy running through it.

What does it want to offer the world?

How does it want to serve the world?

Now place your attention on your mind and your character.

What mental and character traits make you who you are?

How does your mind and personality help you to participate in the world? What are you really good at?

You can also examine the limitations of your mind and character.

What makes it difficult for you to participate in the world?

What has this taught you? How have you grown from it?

How can it help you to show compassion to others?

How can it help you to serve others?

Now listen to your mind and character and the energy running through them.

What do they want to offer the world?

What does the world want to receive from them?

How can you serve the world with the unique gifts you have been given?

Allowing your purpose guide you

You can start with the exercise 2.5.3 on relaxing into the flow of that which is greater. Be fully present with yourself as you examine where you have been finding purpose in life.

What have you been living for?

Is this in line with your heart's values?

Is this what the world wants from you?

Are you serving the world with the unique gifts you have been given?

Notice how pursuing this purpose or these goals has affected who you are and how you show up in the world.

Is this who you want to be?

Now just be still and listen to the energy within and around you. You might want to say these words out loud,

"I'm here to serve. Please show me how I can serve."

Feel these words enter into the core of your being. Allow their intentions to sink into every cell of your being.

You are here to serve.

In what ways can you give this healing back to the world?

Begin to watch through your daily life for all the ways you can give the positive energies you are cultivating back to the world around you.

When we live from the heart, we see every experience as an opportunity to learn, grow, and transform. We then use that growth and transformation to serve the world around us. Life itself becomes our teacher and we become the means for those teachings to spread to the world. The spirit is healed when it no longer clings to one state of being but flows with the energy of life trusting and surrendering into service of this greater system.

PART 3

Building a Foundation of Peace

Healing must be maintained and nurtured. We cannot expect that once we have healed, our well-being will remain no matter what we do. We have to find a way of living in the world that constantly cultivates and waters our well-being. The energies that we feed are the ones that grow. By constantly paying attention to and engaging with feelings of peace, love, compassion, and kindness, we grow a strong foundation. If our foundation is strong, the negative influences of the outside world won't have as large of an impact on us.

6

Mindfulness as a Lifestyle

The practice of looking deeply into the nature of things and how we relate to them does not only happen on a meditation cushion. It is something that we bring into every moment of our lives. It's how we show up in the world. Turning the practice into our lifestyle keeps us engaged with the positive energies of healing at every moment of every day.

We can engage with any activity mindfully. We do this by bringing our attention and intention to whatever it is that we are doing: washing the dishes, driving our car, speaking with a loved one, or working. Attention helps us to be aware of all of the sensations of the experience. What does it sound like, feel like, look like, and smell like? Each tiny detail of the experience becomes a miraculous gift of life that gives us a deeper look into the meaning and depth of all things. A mundane task can become a dynamic examination of life itself. Intention means that we engage with each activity as the best version of ourselves. Our attitude and outlook create thoughts, words, and actions that align with our values. We spend every moment of the day creating a curious and accepting relationship with all experience. Every experience is an opportunity for us to develop our character and transcend self.

While we move through our day, we are constantly aware of our thoughts and what reactions they are creating. We check in with our internal state to recognize our emotions and how they are affecting who we are being. These little check-ins happen consistently. It may help to set a mindful bell alarm on your phone that sounds every hour reminding you to stop, breathe, check in with your internal state, and examine if you were approaching the activity at hand in mindful awareness. Are you living with intention in this moment? Are you using this moment to grow, learn, and transform? Even when we think we do not have the time to be mindful, we can be mindful of our rushing. We can observe what it is like to be in a hurry and the effect it has on our mind and body. We can also observe what it is like not to be aware of what we are doing. What does it feel like when we complete a task and don't remember how we did it? This too is being mindful.

You can use the following exercise to get in touch with what it looks like to live each moment mindfully.

3.6.1 EXERCISE ON MAKING MINDFULNESS A LIFESTYLE

Living mindfully

You can begin with a breathing and centering exercise. Come back to the present moment in non-judgmental awareness. Clear your mind of the need to fix, control, or solve. Become the curious observer.

In this open and aware state of mind, run through your daily routine and focus on one habitual activity that you do regularly. Notice how you engage with this activity.

What is your mental state while you are doing it?

What is your attitude towards the activity?

Are you fully engaged with the task?

What are you thinking while doing the task?

Are you approaching it with intention?

Now come back to your breath and take yourself back to the moment right before you are going to begin this activity. Before you begin, stop, breathe, check in with your internal state, and set some intentions for approaching the activity mindfully.

Imagine yourself moving through the activity.

notice everything that you are hearing.

What sounds do your actions make?

What sounds are going on in your environment?

Notice all of the smells present.

Notice all of the feelings present.

Notice what it looks like, all of the colors, shadows, contrasts, angles, shapes, and dimensions.

Observe your thoughts.

What are you thinking about the activity?

What reactions are these thoughts creating?

What emotions are present?

How are these emotions changing the way that you engage with the world? What are you learning about self and your place in the world?

Are you being who you want to be and engaging with the world the way you want to?

When we live mindfully, we create a relationship of peace and acceptance with every experience. We no longer fight the experiences we are having but engage with them in curiosity so that we can use them for growth and transformation. Our life becomes our practice.

7

The Power of Perspective

In order to build a sturdy foundation, we must first make peace with ourselves and the world. If we carry peace within ourselves, we can feel it anywhere we go. We have to make peace with the way the world is. As Ajahn Brahn says, "there is nothing wrong with you or with the world. The problem is the relationship between the two."[1] Our experience of the world is based on the energies that we are feeding within it. If we think that the world is a horrible place filled with hatred and anger, then we probably live with a lot of hatred and anger within us. In order to live in a world that is peaceful and loving, we have to hold peace and love within ourselves.

Making peace with the world means finding the sources of happiness that are already within and around you and placing all of your attention and intention on them so that they grow and spread outward. If you spend all of your time focusing on what is absent in or wrong with the world, then you are stuck in a dark cave of despair. You can only see what is not good. Come out of your cave and look for all the beauty that already exists. It is there, you just have to engage with it. Even in the darkest of times, there is the possibility for growth and learning.

The first step to making peace with the world is to notice what relationship you have with it and where you're placing your attention. If you are focusing only on what is wrong with the world, then switch your focus. Constantly search for the things that are going well, the things that are beautiful, the love that exists, and the connections being made.

You can use the following exercise to become aware of how you see the world.

3.7.1 EXERCISE ON BECOMING AWARE OF HOW YOU SEE THE WORLD

How do you relate to the world

You can begin with a breathing exercise and coming back home to self. Once you are connected back with self and centered in your heart space, begin to observe your relationship to the world.

How do you see the environment around you?

What labels do you put on it?

How do you feel about the state of your society and other countries?

What thoughts do you have about other people?

What are you seeing around you?

What are you hearing from people and the media?

How are you engaging with the world?

Notice what energies this relationship is cultivating.

Are you feeding love and compassion or are you feeding anger, hatred, and fear?

Notice how this perspective affects who you are being.

Does looking at the world in this way make you a pleasant person?

Are you able to contribute positive energies?

Notice who you are being when you are living with this perspective.

Are you aggressive, fighting, and judging?

Are these the energies you want to see in the world?

What are you offering the world?

With this perspective are you able to offer love, compassion, and acceptance?

Now allow your mind to open and ask yourself, who do I want to be and how do I want to see the world?

Choosing to see the energies you want to cultivate

This exercise can be done after the previous one or following a breathing and connecting exercise. Center yourself in your heart space. Connect with who you want to be and what energies you want to cultivate.

Get in touch with your current environment.

How would you like to be experiencing this environment?

What do you want to see in your environment?

What would you like to hear?

What do you want to feel?

How would this environment be if you were feeling peace, love, and compassion?

Now place yourself out in the world. This can be anywhere that you go frequently. Ask yourself the same questions. How do you want to experience the world?

Look around with intention. Imagine all of the manifestations of what you wanted to experience in the world lighting up around you as the negative ones fade into the background.

Surround yourself with the presence of these positive energies. Notice how as you focus on them more and more appear.

Notice how your whole surroundings become these energies. Allow them to grow and spread outward. Imagine yourself engaging with these energies, feeding them and adding to them.

How does it feel to be engaged in the world in this way?

Who are you being?

What are you able to offer the world?

As we engage more and more with the positive energies around us, we have less and less to resist and fight. The positive grows and the negative fades without us having to fight against it. When we stop resisting what life has to offer, we can engage with the good that's already present. Eckhart Tolle states that "Only if you resist what happens are you at the mercy of what happens, and the world will determine your happiness and unhappiness."[37]

We suffer when we refuse to accept the realities of life. As Thich Nhat Hanh says, "If we accept life and everything that belongs to life - the moments of happiness, joy, and peace, but also sickness, old age, and death - then we don't suffer anymore."[18] Fighting with the world is what causes us pain. As humans we are of the nature to disappoint one another, to hurt one another, to get sick, to die, to get old, and slowly lose our ability to function. Denying this only gives us false expectations that disappoint us. We cannot avoid the natural sufferings of life; the only thing we can do is cultivate the good through them.

Making peace with the world means accepting what is while engaging fully with the energies we want to manifest so that they grow even when surrounded by difficulty. There is always a potential for love, compassion, and peace; we just have to find it within ourselves. As Victor Frankl says, "When we cannot change our situation we are challenged to change ourselves."[16] There is no tragedy too great to be transformed into a personal triumph and a transformative power for humanity."

You can make peace with the world by noticing the experiences that you resist and transforming the fight into an expression of love and compassion. This will lead to personal transformation.

3.7.2 EXERCISES ON TURNING RESISTANCE INTO GROWTH

Recognizing your resistance

You can begin with a breathing exercise and coming back home to self. Center in your heart space as you open into observation of your relationship with the current situations in your life.

Scan through all of the experiences present for you today or this week. Is there one that feels uncomfortable, negative, or challenging? Observe how you react to this situation.

When you think about a certain situation, how does your body respond? What tightens?

What hurts?

Where do you feel it?

Does your head pound?

What is your heart feeling?

Where does your energy go?

Now observe how you are reacting in your mind.

What is your perspective of it?

What are you telling yourself about this situation?

How are you relating to it?

What is your attitude towards it?

How are you reacting?

Are you fighting and resisting?

What are you wanting to be different?

Why do you think this needs to be different?

What would it offer you if it were different?

How is this affecting who you are being and how you are showing up in the world?

What does resistance look like in your body?

In your mind?

In how you are interacting with others?

What are you saying and doing while resisting life and the experience?

Who do you want to be?

What do you want to offer the world?

What attitude could you adopt towards this situation to cultivate the energies you want to share with the world?

Moving from resistance to transformation

This exercise can follow the previous one or be done after a breathing exercise and coming back to self. Center in your heart space, connecting with who you want to be and the energies you want to share with the world.

Welcome into your awareness a difficult situation present in your life. From this place of being grounded in the positive energies, begin to observe the nature of the situation.

What is difficult about it?

What am I trying to change?

What am I trying not to feel?

What am I trying to avoid?

Why don't I want to experience these things?

Am I afraid that it will threaten me or that I won't get one of my needs met?

Remember your true sources of all of these needs. They are always present within and around you. You just have to engage with them. Engage with these centering energies and ask yourself.

How can I stay true to myself and my heart values even while experiencing this situation?

How can I learn from this experience?

How can I grow from this experience?

What does this tell me about what I need to seek out in life?

What is this telling me about how I need to transform within myself so that I don't get trapped in the negativity, the new skills I need to develop, or what resources I need to find?

Set an intention for yourself to seek out the resources that will help you to use this situation as an opportunity for transformation.

Imagine who you can become if you use this situation as a personal triumph and a transformative power for the world.

Remember that nothing happens to you, it always happens for you.

Why is this experience happening for you?

We create our relationship with the world. We can choose to resist what happens by fighting or we can choose to make peace with what is and form a healthy relationship with life.

8

Forgiving Self and Others

Forgiveness is essential to turning a difficult situation into an opportunity for transformation. In order to fully embrace and live out the lessons taught by suffering, we have to fully forgive the original cause. Sometimes teaching us the ability to forgive is the main reason for our experience of difficulty. If we don't learn the basic teaching of forgiveness, then we will not continue to move down our path of transformation.

In order to forgive others, we must first recognize the same human afflictions within ourselves and forgive them. If we hold ourselves up on a pedestal of perfection, then we are blind to our own shortcomings, but recognize them readily in others. When we lack the ability to forgive, we have a very hard time admitting our own faults, and when we find fault in others, we hold it over their heads forever. By finding humility, we recognize that we are just as vulnerable and flawed as all other humans and are just as worthy of forgiveness.

Forgiveness of self is a process of admitting our weaknesses, accepting them, and then letting go of resentment towards these weaknesses as we work towards healing the wrong we have done because of them. It does not mean that we excuse all of our harmful actions; it means we don't hold onto them and allow them to eat away at our well-being. We understand that there is a lot more to us than any one of our faults or mistakes. By recognizing our own weaknesses, we are able to grow compassion and understanding for others. We understand the powerful afflictions that others face and how hard it is to never allow our weaknesses to manifest as negative thoughts, words, and actions. This helps us to forgive others when their weaknesses manifest as negative thoughts, words, and actions that harm us.

Through forgiveness, our weaknesses can become our strengths and we transform their energy into something useful. For example, I have the tendency to be very stubborn. I understand that this trait can manifest as the need to control others, denying their right to a perspective, which cuts me off from receiving their wisdom and help. The harder I try to deny and suppress this trait in me, the worse it becomes. If instead I am able to recognize my stubbornness, accept it, and understand its purpose, then I can transform it into something useful. I can use the positive energies of this characteristic as determination and resilience, keeping me moving towards a worthy cause while remaining open to others.

You can use the following exercises to help you get in touch with your own weaknesses and forgive them so that they can become your strengths.

3.8.1 EXERCISES ON FORGIVING OUR WEAKNESS

Recognizing and accepting your weaknesses

You can begin with a breathing exercise and then come back home to your heart-space. Recognize your heart's true nature to accept, forgive, and love all things.

Trust your heart's ability to hold anything that you find within yourself in compassion. There is nothing within you that is unworthy of forgiveness or unable to be transformed.

Open yourself into truth. Look at yourself honestly. Know that every living being has within them the light and the dark, the good and the bad, the difficult and the easy. This is what makes us a beautiful complex being capable of understanding and showing compassion to others who also have weaknesses.

What are your greatest weaknesses?

How do you harm others?

How do you harm yourself?

Listen to what you are telling yourself about these weaknesses.

Are these words loving and kind?

Do these words help you to heal or do they build more anger and contempt?

Soften your words towards your weaknesses. Admit that you have faults and lay them open for your heart or your God to see. These are a part of who you are. There is no part of you too ugly to be held within the heart.

Accept that you have weaknesses.

Accept that you are human and flawed.

Trust the heart to hold this truth with compassion.

Open yourself to forgiveness.

Say these words out loud, "Although I am flawed, I am worthy of love. I am worthy of forgiveness. I can forgive myself."

Transforming your weaknesses into compassion and strength

This exercise can follow the previous one or be done on its own after a breathing exercise and coming back home to the loving safety of the heart.

Recognize your weaknesses with compassion. Notice how they show up in your life.

How do they manifest in your thoughts, words, and actions?

Who have they hurt?

How strong of a hold do these weaknesses have on you?

How hard is it to not allow them to harm you or others?

This is how hard it is for others not to allow their weaknesses to harm you. Can you see their afflictions within you and yours within them?

You share the same basic human weaknesses. All humans make mistakes. Feel your compassion growing for the weaknesses of others.

Now hold your weakness close. Look at the energies behind the negative thoughts, words, and actions.

Is there a positive force here?

Can you use these energies to do good?

How could this weakness become a strength?

For example, anger could be seen as recognition of the negative in the world and motivation to change it. Our indignation could be used as the energy to create more good in the world. Our lack of organization may just be a manifestation of our creative side needing to break free.

Imagine yourself recognizing the energies of your weakness before they manifest into negative behaviors and transforming them into something good.

What are you able to do?

Who are you able to be?

What are you able to offer the world?

Harness the good energy from your weakness and hold it within your heart and core. This is your human potential to transform weakness into strength.

Forgiveness of self becomes easier if we get in touch with and heal our inner child. Most of our destructive behaviors and beliefs began when we were children, at a time when we did not have the tools or understanding necessary to nurture ourselves and take care of our own well-being. We were at the mercy of our caretakers, which leaves us very vulnerable and impressionable. If we were unsafe during this time and did not have an outlet for our hurts and fears, then we most likely stored them within our body, mind, and spirit. If we have not healed these wounds, then they are still present within us, creating the fuel for our emotional reactions and destructive behavior. These unhealed wounds are sometimes referred to as our pain body. They are the soft spots that become our trigger points.

Instead of judging ourselves for our hurtful and destructive behavior, we can bring compassion to it by bringing compassion to this inner child who did not have the ability to take care of her/himself when the wounding happened. When we were children, we had not yet developed healthy ways of dealing with hardship. We could not turn to the tools of self-care that we have now to ensure our own well-being, so we reacted to hurtful behavior by trying to manipulate, avoid, or attack the person hurting us. If we have not listened to and healed this inner child in the process of developing healthy ways to care for self, then we are probably still manipulating, avoiding, or attacking anyone who triggers our pain body today.

We can begin to heal from these early woundings by recognizing what our inner child is afraid of, and what he/she is trying to protect herself against. We can go back to when we were children and look into the fears we felt and which of our basic needs felt threatened. If these fears and unmet needs were not nurtured and healed, then they probably got stored somewhere in the body, the mind, or the spirit. The places that we store them in the body are usually the first to get injured or experience tension and pain. The mind stores these fears and hurts as harmful perspectives of self, of the world, or of others. The spirit holds them as religious anger or spiritual disconnect. These then become our trigger points for pain that lead us into our defense behavior.

Instead of believing the stories of these pain bodies, we can simply hold them in love and reassure them that now we have the tools necessary to stay safe and whole even in difficult situations. We can tell our inner child that they no longer have to protect us and that we have the ability to keep ourselves well. We can forgive our inner child for not having the tools or understanding to take care of themselves, and that we understand why they developed those defense behaviors. But we reassure that inner child that he/she no longer needs those behaviors to stay safe. We now have the ability to stay true to ourselves and take care of our well-being without those destructive habits.

3.8.2 EXERCISES ON RELATING TO THE INNER CHILD

Noticing how the inner child reacts

You can begin with a breathing and centering exercise. Come back to self and become aware of your body, mind and spirit. Stay present with self as you bring your inner child into your awareness.

Ask your inner child what they were afraid of.

Which of their needs weren't met?

You may recall a specific hurtful event or just the overall perspective of the child. Observe what they perceived as a threat. Notice what they were feeling. Feel their vulnerability. Recognize how impressionable they were. Observe how they responded to the hurtful experience or to hurt in general.

Where did it manifest within the body?

What perspectives of self, the world, or other did it generate?

What disconnect did it create in the spirit?

Where did they turn for help?

If there was no help where did they store the pain?

Is it still there today?

This child is you so wherever they stored their pain if it hasn't been healed, it is still there. How did the child react?

Did they manipulate, avoid, or attack?

Is this behavior still present in you today?

If you have not recognized this pain body, healed it, and developed healthier ways of taking care of your well-being, then these defense behaviors are still present. They may always be your first reaction.

Notice if they worked for the child and if the child healed. Notice if these behaviors work for you today if they help you heal today.

Tell the inner child that it's time to move away from these behaviors. Move towards your healthy adult self.

From a healthy place, choose a response rather than defaulting to these defense reactions.

Forgiving the inner child

You can do this exercise after you have recognized the ways your inner child has stored pain and still reacts to it. Bring this child into your awareness.

Hold your inner child within the warm, loving, and accepting space of your heart. Show up for your child as your adult self who knows all of the resources available to nurture and heal.

Share with your inner child your understanding of their pain and the defense behaviors they developed to protect themselves against it.

Tell them that you understand why they had to do that and that you don't judge them for it. Tell them how sorry you are that they had no other choice at the time.

Remind them that they were young and vulnerable and had not developed any other way to take care of themselves.

Hug their pain in the embrace of your love. Tell them that you forgive them for developing those pain bodies and defense behaviors.

Forgive them for the hurt they felt when they could not take care of themselves.

Forgive them for hurting others with their defense behavior.

Reassure them they no longer need these harmful defense behaviors.

Know that you are now strong and balanced, and have developed healthy ways of taking care of your well-being.

Tell them that you are here for them and that everything will be okay.

Once we have forgiven ourselves, we have to forgive life and the suffering it carries. Forgiving and learning from tragedy does not mean that we deny ourselves the right to feel the sadness, anger, and fear that it evokes. Part of the learning process involves feeling all of these emotions fully and then moving through them towards healing. We suffer less while going through this process if we do not spend energy blaming life for treating us unfairly. Life is not out to get you. It is not plotting against you. It is simply being what it is: a roller coaster of ups and downs filled with happiness, love, suffering, and loss. No one can avoid the tragedies of life; eventually they touch us all. When we move away from being the victim of our suffering, we can begin to use it for growth.

When tragedy strikes, it is very common to ask "why me" as though you should for some reason be exempt from the natural suffering of life. Instead of asking "why me," try asking "what do I need to learn from this?" Getting in touch with the teachings offered by a tragedy makes it easier for us to forgive the initial cause. This is often true of survivors of near death experiences or grave illnesses. They say that they wouldn't be who they are without that experience and wouldn't trade it for anything.

Once we realize how much growth has come from our experience, our perspective of it changes; we begin to thank it rather than resent it.

This does not mean that we don't allow ourselves to feel the suffering of our hardship or undesired situation. We do need to move through the whole process of being with what is happening and admitting how hard it is for us. This is the work we did in the sections on healing the body, the mind, and the spirit and in the section on emotions. All of this work allows us to recognize what is difficult in life and soften it. We allow ourselves to feel the whole spectrum of emotions without denying or avoiding. But once we have fully felt the experience, it is time to forgive and move forward. Holding onto resentment for life's hardships only leaves us bitter and stuck. Forgiving helps us to transition through the suffering into the growth and learning.

You can begin your process of forgiving the suffering of life with the following exercises.

3.8.3 EXERCISES ON FORGIVING THE SUFFERING OF LIFE

Accepting suffering

Begin with a breathing exercise and coming back home to self. Get in touch with the suffering present in your life. It may be a past experience or one present now.

First explore how the suffering feels in your body.

Where are you carrying the suffering?

Where is your body resisting it?

What does the suffering do to your energy levels?

Now explore the suffering in your mind.

What feelings are behind your suffering?

Where do you feel them?

What are you telling yourself about the situation?

Are you trying to resist the experience?

Did you have expectations that nothing bad should happen to you?

Do you feel like a victim?

Now soften to the experience. Remind yourself that suffering is a natural occurrence of life. Remind yourself that you are not being treated unfairly. Remind yourself that you are not a victim.

Take your suffering back. Own it and decide what to do with it.

How do you want to use this suffering to grow and transform?

Who do you want to be during your suffering and once you heal from it?

Imagine yourself being this person.

Empower yourself to be this person.

Forgiving suffering so we can learn from it

This exercise can follow the previous one or be done on its own after a breathing and centering exercise. Get in touch with the suffering present in your life. It may be a past experience or one present now.

Soften to your suffering and remember that you are not a victim. Step into your empowered self and ask this situation what it is trying to teach you. Look into the situation and the challenges it presents to you.

What skills, qualities, or insights are present within the struggle?

What weaknesses is it challenging?

What opportunities for growth is it presenting you with?

Maybe it is helping you to develop new ways of relating to your body with peace and compassion. Maybe it is showing you old perspectives and stories that need to shift for you to see the world positively. Maybe it is showing you the ways you resist vulnerability, love, and support out of fear or pride. Allow it to show you your own weaknesses and open your heart to the possibility of growth through them.

Imagine who you can become if you own the lessons and use them for good. Get in touch with the person who has used this suffering to create beauty and possibility.

What does this person think about the original situation?

Is this person angry and resentful?

Is this person able to forgive?

Now recognize this person within you and get in touch with the forgiveness.

Soften to your suffering and forgive life for presenting you with this challenge. Now move forward towards your transformation.

If our suffering was caused by an individual or a group of people, then we have to forgive them. Forgiveness does not mean that we excuse or deny the actions that caused our suffering. It means that we don't hold onto resentment and anger. Rather than looking at it as setting the perpetrator free from blame and responsibility, look at it as setting yourself free of anger and resentment. In forgiveness, we do not have to become friends with our perpetrator and invite them back into our lives. We just stop spending energy on hating them and blaming them. I myself have spent many years forgiving my father and my brother for their anger and emotional abuse used to control the people in their lives. Although I have found compassion for them and forgiven them for how they hurt me, I still do not see them often out of compassion for myself. I recognize the toll their presence takes on my well-being. I know that subjecting myself to their harmful behavior only creates more anger, harming both of us. The choice to take care of myself by distancing myself from them empowered me and helped me to grow and learn many important skills. This is why I do not blame them or hate them. I know that what I went through with them helped me to become the person I am today. Jack Kornfield explains this well by saying, "Forgiveness does not ignore the truth of our suffering. Forgiveness is not weak. It demands courage and integrity. Yet only forgiveness and love can bring about the peace we long for."[25]

Forgiveness begins with finding compassion for self and our perpetrator. We already prepared ourselves for this by recognizing that the same weaknesses that lead to negative thoughts, words, and actions exist within us as well as in our perpetrator. We are all flawed humans and we all fall victim to our inability to heal our traumas, wounds, and vulnerabilities leading to harmful behavior. We found compassion for ourselves by forgiving our own shortcomings and flaws. Now we can find compassion for those who have harmed us.

Getting in touch with the deep rooted suffering responsible for the actions of our perpetrator can help us to soften our hatred. We can get in touch with this person's inner child understanding they too were once young, vulnerable, and impressionable and that they probably faced much hurt and trauma during that time which has not been healed. We see that their hurtful behavior comes from these painful bodies and we feel compassion for their inability to move past the destructive reactions of their wounded child. For example, my dad grew up in a military family, always moving to new countries never knowing if his dad would be alive by dinner. His mom was very resentful of their situation and treated him with the same emotional abuse that he now shows me. Understanding this helps me to keep myself safe while softening my heart to his flaws.

Again, this does not excuse our perpetrator for their actions, but simply helps us not to take their harmful behavior too personally. We were simply an outlet for the suffering they themselves felt. The best way to prevent them from continuing these harmful acts is to help them heal. We can do this by forgiving them and sending them loving kindness destined to rid them of the blind spots that lead to hatred, anger, aggression, and division. This can be done without any contact with the actual person.

You can use the following exercises to begin forgiving those who have harmed you.

3.8.4 EXERCISES ON FINDING COMPASSION FOR THOSE WHO HAVE HURT YOU

Recognizing what we need to forgive

You can begin with a breathing and centering exercise. Then follow the breath into the body. Stay with the body as you ask it if it is holding any anger, hatred, or resentment towards anyone.

Scan the body and notice where there is tension: pain in the body, tension in your muscles, fatigue, headaches, or illness. You can place a hand on this area and allow the hand to carry the energies of the heart right to this pain in the body. Let it know you are ready to listen.

Ask it what it is holding onto.

Listen to the story you are telling yourself about what this person or group of people did to make you suffer.

Notice what role you think they played in the experience and what role you played.

Are you making yourself the victim?

Ask it who you are blaming for the pain.

Feel what energies you are storing here.

What feelings are present?

Are you angry or resentful towards a specific person for causing these feelings?

Why are you holding onto this story?

Do you think it will protect you from future hurt?

Do you think it will bring you revenge or justice?

Notice what holding onto this pain story is actually doing to your body, mind, and spirit. Notice who it is turning you into. Notice that it is only harming you and that in turn you end up harming the people you love.

Are you ready to heal?

Ask it what it needs in order to heal.

This person or group of people need your forgiveness.

Notice how simply holding the intentions to forgive begins to soften the pain in your heart and body. You become a bit softer and lighter. You can start returning to who your really are. A person of love, compassion, peace, acceptance, and gratitude.

Working through forgiveness

This exercise can be done after the previous one or after a breathing and centering exercise. Bring into your awareness the person that you need to forgive. Notice how you see them when you are looking through your lens of hatred and resentment.

Who are you making them out to be?

What do they look like?

What are they saying?

What are they doing?

Now come into your heart space and center here in love, compassion, and kindness. Open your heart to seeing this person from a place of compassion. See this person as an equal human being who has also been hurt and battered by life.

Notice their weaknesses and how they manifest into negative

thoughts, words, and actions. Notice how hurtful it is to this person to act the way they do.

See their inner child and all of the pain that child stored within their mind, body, and spirit, and all the defense behavior it developed to stay safe.

Now look within yourself and get in touch with your own weaknesses, hurts, fears, and vulnerabilities.

Do you share some of the same ones?

Who do you become when you act out of them?

What do you need in order to feel safe and at peace?

Offer the same compassion to the person who hurt you. Know that they hurt others because they are hurting deeply within themselves.

Forgive them for hurting you.

Look into their heart and ask it why it's hurting.

Ask it how it has suffered and how long it has gone un-nurtured.

Ask it what it's afraid of and why it feels so vulnerable.

Send them love and kindness and the wish that they are able to heal their suffering and see through their blind spots so that they stop harming others.

Picture them receiving whatever it is that they need for healing. Notice how you feel after forgiving. Notice how it feels to live in compassion.

Once we have reconnected with our compassion for the other person, we have to become aware of what anger, resentment and blame we are holding onto and why. Sometimes we believe that this anger and hatred act as the armor that will protect us from ever getting hurt again. But what we fail to realize is that this armor actually prevents us from loving ourselves and others, and it may end up creating destructive behaviors that lead us to harm others in the same way that we ourselves were harmed. When I began the healing process after separating from my family, I held on to my anger as though it were a badge of honor that would protect me from this ever happening again. What it actually did was build a wall between me and everyone that could have loved me. I was self-destructive, and carried a self-image that attracted more people with the same energy as my dad and brother. It wasn't until I let go of this anger and took down my walls that I could let my heart open to healing.

We may believe that this anger is giving us the power to fight back and make a difference. In the short term, anger can be useful. It points to something that needs addressing in our life and gives us the motivation to change it. But if we stay in anger past the point of recognition it becomes destructive. Healing never takes place in anger. Long term anger drains us of our life force and prevents us from moving forward into peace and love where we experience healing and rejuvenation. As Martin Luther King stated, "Hatred cannot heal hatred, only love can do that." Anger notifies us that we need to make a change but once we are notified we need to switch gears and act out of love.

If we are holding onto anger, we are probably stuck in a victim mentality. We can start moving out of anger by recognizing what story of victimhood we are holding onto. Do you tell yourself over and over that you have been wronged and that you deserve to be angry about it? Notice what perceptions you carry of self, the world, and others because of this victimhood. When we hold onto anger and blame, we usually label others and the world as unsafe or cruel. This makes it very difficult to reach out in love and connect with others.

We can begin to recognize how carrying hatred and resentment affects our lives. Who do we become when we harbor hatred? Most likely, we start to share a lot of the same characteristics as our perpetrator, and may even hurt others in the same way we were hurt. Hatred and resentment eat away at our body, soul, and mind. They deteriorate our well-being and disconnect us from the beauty of life. The longer we identify with our pain and hatred, the more they become who we are. Letting go of hatred and resentment does not make us weak, it makes us beautiful and strong. It allows us to re-engage with the world in peace.

3.8.5 EXERCISES ON LETTING GO OF ANGER, RESENTMENT, AND BLAME

Letting go of negative feelings

Begin with the exercise on recognizing what we need to forgive. Then follow the breath up into the mind space and explore where you store feelings of anger, resentment, and blame.

What are these stored energies and feelings doing to the body?

Maybe they are tension in the shoulders, acidity in the digestive track, pain in the spine or neck, fatigue.

What are these stored energies and feelings doing to the mind?

What perspective of the world and the other do they give you?

What perspective of self do you have when you're looking through their lens? Is there a feeling of being a victim?

While you are absorbed in these energies and thoughts, who are you being? How do you treat others?

What are you spending your energy on?

If you are spending your energy hating, resenting, or blaming someone, then this is the person you need to forgive.

Imagine yourself releasing this stored up hatred and resentment in your body. Imagine that space of anger within the body beginning to release and let go. Imagine the light of love and healing shining into it and forcing it to break apart as it absorbs back into your wholeness returning you to who you truly are. Returning the body back to its healthy form.

Imagine yourself releasing this stored up hatred and resentment in your mind. Allow it to soften within you. Imagine that light of love and healing shining into that dark space within the mind where you have that anger stored away and clear it out leaving nothing but wide open beautiful space. Picture that hatred flowing out of your mind and body leaving you light and free.

Turn towards the energies within your heart: love, compassion, peace, forgiveness. Feed these energies instead of hatred and resentment.

Now notice who you are being and how you are interacting with the world. Who can you be when you are free from resentment and anger?

What can you offer the world?

Once we have done the work of forgiveness, we can set the perpetrator free by telling them. If being in contact with the perpetrator puts you in danger or compromises your well-being, then just write a letter and keep it for yourself. If not, then you can decide if you would rather express your forgiveness in a sent letter or in person. This is a very deep act of compassion towards this person, so do not do it until you have forgiven them with all your heart. Speaking your forgiveness will set you free from the spell of anger, and it will set them free from identifying with their wrong-doing. You are not taking away their responsibility, you are simply giving them the freedom to begin anew. If you forever label them as a wrong-doer, then that is what they will become. Tell them that you see them as so much more than one of their mistakes. Set them free to live out their potential.

If you live with this person, then this step is very important. Without it, you will both go on living out the hurt of the past, one person feeling guilty and the other feeling like a victim. This is unconducive to a healthy relationship. No real connection can develop between a wrong-doer and their victim. True intimacy is always between equals. Forgiveness tells your loved one that you consider them an equal and they no longer have to pay for their mistake in order to be accepted.

If this person's mistakes are very frequent and always of the same aggressive nature, then your forgiveness should happen without their presence in your life. You can offer them the freedom to become something better without being present for it. Never stay in a situation that is compromising your well-being.

Once you have forgiven someone, you can no longer hold the event over their head when something else arises in your relationship. This mistake is now released from the vault of ammunition for disagreements. If you use it against them later, then your forgiveness is not genuine and will have to be worked through again.

This step is what takes the healing that you have done within you and shares it out with the world healing others. Tara Brach tells a story in her dharma about a mother who lost her son to a gang shooting. The boy who shot her son was sentenced to prison, and as he was leaving the courtroom, she told him that she would kill him. A few months into his prison sentence, this mother went to visit him. She said that she was working on forgiveness and needed to see him in person to move through her anger. She visited him once a week for the rest of his sentence. She would bring him books and teach him new skills. They talked about his past and how he ended up where he was. He had had a traumatic childhood and was left to fend for himself, so the gang was his only family. When he was released from prison, the mother invited him to stay with her until he got on his feet. She gave him clothes to wear, fed him, and helped him to find a job. Once he was settled in his new job and had a stable life free of the gang, she asked him if he remembered the day she had told him she would kill him. She said that now she had. That boy who had killed her son was dead, and he had begun anew as a young man with plenty of possibility in front of him. Her ability to forgive not only healed her, but healed a little piece of the whole world.

3.8.6 EXERCISE ON SHARING YOUR FORGIVENESS

How to share your forgiveness

When you are preparing your words of forgiveness, make sure that you are speaking from your heart, not your anger.

Tell the other person how much they mean to you and that your deepest desire is to be able to heal together. Recognize that we must all heal together, that our healing is linked to the healing of others.

Acknowledge that they are so much more than this mistake. That they are so much more than these negative words or actions. That they also have sides of love and compassion.

Recognize that harmful words and actions always stem from internal suffering and express an interest in understanding theirs. Knowing that when you understand one another's sources of suffering that you can do your best not to feed them.

Let them know that you are freeing them from the burden of this mistake and that you are ready to begin anew.

Tell them that they no longer have to pay for their mistake in order to be accepted, because you have forgiven them.

Connect with them from the heart seeing and believing who they are at their core. They are love. Come back to your love for them.

Healing through forgiveness requires us to ask for forgiveness from the people we have hurt. There is not one of us who has lived our whole life without harming another human being or the planet. Even if we do not do so intentionally, our blind spots and weaknesses lead us to treat others carelessly. We may not even be aware that we have done it until the person tells us. When our own harmful behavior is brought to our attention, we must listen with an open heart and mind. This is very difficult if we don't believe that we make mistakes. Our ego has to soften so that we are able to see ourselves as imperfect. Yes, we are capable of harming others.

Once our ego is softened and we are open to hearing how our words or actions have harmed someone else, we can ask the other person to share their experience with us. Even if what the other person says does not align with how we remember the situation, we can listen to their perspective. This is how they experienced it. We try to experience our words and actions through their eyes. Listen to how it affected them. We try to avoid justifying our actions with their behavior. No matter what someone has done to us, it does not give us permission to treat them poorly.

It can be very difficult to be confronted with our own weaknesses. That is why we do the work of recognizing our own hurts and vulnerabilities so that we better understand why we act carelessly. When we get in touch with our own suffering, we recognize and acknowledge that we are capable of causing suffering in others. It does not make us a horrible human being, it just means we make mistakes. The first step to healing is awareness. Look into your suffering and understand how it manifests in your words and actions. Set intentions for how you can consistently work towards healing these so that your harmful behavior doesn't continue. These wounds do not justify poor behavior, they help us to understand why we harm others and how to begin healing.

Once we have fully understood how we have harmed the other person, we ask for forgiveness. This can be in a letter or in person. If you hurt this person to the point that it would compromise their well-being to be in your presence, then just write a letter.

While I was caught in my anger and victimhood from my past I hurt many people. I was so focused on my own pain that I didn't recognize what I was doing to others. As I began to heal, I started to see all the ways that I had projected my pain onto others, causing the same wound in them. Asking for forgiveness did not bring the relationship back to where it was before the hurt, but it did validate the pain those individuals had experienced and offered them the opportunity to free themselves from the story. It also helped me to grow and learn so that I am more aware of how to be a safe person for others to be around.

3.8.7 EXERCISE IN ASKING FOR FORGIVENESS

Engaging with humility

You can start with a breathing and centering exercise. Once you are grounded in mind, body, and spirit you can ask yourself the question,

"Have I ever harmed the earth or other beings?"

Notice your reaction to this question.

Do you want to deny that you do harm?

Do you want to justify your harmful actions?

Do you blame others for your behavior?

Soften all of these self-protection mechanisms that keep you from seeing your full humanness. Know that you have harmed other beings and the planet. Notice the ways that you have.

Remember all of the wounds and traumas in your life that lead to your hurtful behavior. You may notice the fears and insecurities behind your behavior. Notice what you were hoping to get by behaving in this way.

Did you do this to protect yourself?

Did you do this to protect your pride or your ego?

Did you do this get love, belonging or acceptance?

Remember that everyone has these afflictions.

Don't justify your behavior with statements like: I deserve this, everyone does it, they asked for it; instead, understand why it happens. Acknowledge your own weaknesses. Remember what you were trying to get from the behavior.

Bring compassion to your mistakes and shine the light of understanding on them. Humble yourself to admit that you cause harm, destruction, and pain. Come back to your heart's values and who you really want to be.

Forgive yourself.

Ask for forgiveness from the planet, from all living beings, and from the individuals that you have harmed.

Ask for forgiveness

Start by explaining that you care about their well-being and that your intentions are to heal together. Acknowledge how you have made them suffer.

Share your own vulnerability and suffering not as an excuse, but as a way to explain the cause of your actions or words.

Express your desire to heal. Share what you are doing to heal. Ask for their forgiveness so that you can move forward together. Ask them to allow you to begin anew.

Forgiving the world, ourselves, and others brings us the peace necessary to heal. Forgiveness is a choice. We either choose to hold on to the negative energies of anger, resentment, and hatred or we choose to turn towards the light and fill ourselves with peace, love, and compassion. Forgiveness empowers us to live as our best selves and cultivate the healing energies we want to share with the world.

9

Mindful Consumption

A realistic perspective makes it easier for us to forgive and forgiveness allows us to have a peaceful relationship with life. This peace is the foundation for a healthy lifestyle. But our strong foundation can become weak if we consistently consume negative images, foods, beverages, substances, conversations, and environments; we will begin to absorb and become these negative energies. We must be aware of how we interact with the world and what we are absorbing from our environment so that we can continue to share forth positive energies rather than feeding negative ones.

What we choose to surround ourselves with and ingest becomes who we are. Becoming a mindful consumer can help us to absorb what is positive in our environment, allowing us to be the best version of ourselves.

We nourish our minds and bodies in many different ways.

It is important to recognize and show gratitude to all of the forms of nourishment that we receive every day. We may nourish ourselves by eating a good meal, engaging in stimulating conversation, taking a quiet walk in the woods, tending our garden, reading an insightful book, or watching an educational video. There are endless ways that the world can nourish us; we just have to engage with them.

We also need to get in touch with our intentions and notice if what we are consuming aligns with who we want to be. If we are consuming things that leave us feeling unhealthy, angry, hateful, or violent, then we will be unable to show up positively in the world. Look into who you want to be and choose to consume in a way that encourages that version of yourself to appear.

You can use the following exercises to begin exploring your consumption.

3.9.1 EXERCISES ON RECOGNIZING HOW I NOURISH MYSELF

Consuming in ways that nourish me

You can begin with a breathing and centering exercise. First reconnect with the body so that you can observe and listen to it. Notice how the body feels and how it shows up in the world when you are being your heart centered self.

Ask your body what it needs to be nourished.

Ask it what you consume that keeps you aligned with your true self.

Tell the body that your intentions are to take care of it and allow it to be healthy and whole.

Listen to what it needs in order to be healthy and whole. Notice that these things may be different depending on the situation or day.

Now bring your attention up into your mind. Become the observer, not the thinker. Notice what the mind feels like and what state it is in when you are living as your authentic heart centered self. Tell the mind that your intentions are to take care of it so that it can be clear, focused, and healthy.

Ask it what it needs to be healthy and happy. Listen to the forms of nourishment that your mind is asking for.

Ask the mind what you consume that allows it to show up as its best self.

What does it want you to offer it?

Now bring your attention to your heart space and your spirit. Notice how the heart and spirit feel when you are being your authentic heart centered self. Tell your spirit that your intentions are to take care of it so that it can be open to experience, insight, love, and compassion.

Ask it what it needs to be open and healthy.

Ask it what you consume that helps it to show up as its best self.

Listen to the forms of nourishment that your heart and spirit are asking for. What do they want you to offer them?

Set some intentions for how you are going to offer your mind, body, and spirit the forms of nourishment that they need to be healthy and happy.

Who do you want to be?

How do you want to show up in the world?

What do you want to offer the world?

How do you want to interact with the world?

What is most important to you?

What do you value most?

Now look into the way you consume.

Ask the body if there are things you consume that make it harder for the body to show up intentionally.

Do you consume things that take more energy to cleanse than the energy they provide?

Ask the mind if there are things you consume that make it harder for it to show up intentionally.

Do you consume things that make the mind clouded and foggy or that bring in thoughts of anger, judgment or division?

Ask the heart and spirit if there are things you consume that make it harder for them to show up intentionally.

Do you consume things that make the heart and spirit closed off and disconnected?

Is what you choose to absorb from the world helping you to live out your intentions?

Are you consuming in a way that reflects your values?

Are you consuming in a way that allows you to be who you want to be and offer what you want to offer?

Return to your intentions to consume in a way that makes it easier for you to live as your authentic heart centered self. Notice how this creates a trust within you that lessens your need to struggle with consumption. Allow this trust to bring a peace into your whole being and return you to those energies of love, compassion, acceptance, and gratitude.

Food and drink are one form of nourishment. What we ingest becomes who we are. There is no one diet that is best for all beings. Each individual will have a unique diet that fits them best. The key to finding that magic diet is becoming aware of what types of food nourish our mind, body, and spirit. This is not as straightforward as the most recent diet trend. It takes constant observation of and communication with self. Sometimes our spirit might really need a homemade cookie to share with a loved one, warming our heart. The body might need a big leafy salad to cleanse our system and fill us with nutrients. The mind might need fish to stimulate its cognitive processing. Our dietary needs will also change with age and circumstance. Certain illnesses may require dietary changes that weren't necessary otherwise. Each day we will need to ask ourselves if we are eating in a way that nourishes our mind, body, and spirit.

Eating for the spirit means that we are eating in a way that aligns with our values and intentions. If we have intentions for peace and compassion we may not want to consume things that harm animals or our planet. If we value sustainability and our local community, then we may want to eat as many regional products as possible. When our consumption habits match our values, we have a much more peaceful relationship with food and digest it a lot better.

Eating for the body means that we listen to what our body needs to be healthy. This may change by the day. If we have done a lot of strenuous work, we may need to eat fattier, heartier meals. If we feel heavy and lethargic, we may need to eat a lot of vegetables and fruit. This also depends on our body type and lifestyle. The body will tell you if you are consuming things that aren't good for it. You won't feel very well and you will need to listen to what it is you should avoid. If you feel sick, tired, bloated, or lethargic after eating something, then don't eat it.

Eating for the mind means that we listen to what the mind

needs to be clear and focused. Try to avoid products that cloud your judgment, fog your mind, or make you unsettled. We need a healthy mind in order to gain insight and wisdom. Notice how what you put in your body affects your mind, and consume in a way that helps the mind to remain open and healthy.

After learning about the interconnectedness of all things and how I take in the energies of what I eat, I decided to become a vegetarian. I knew that based on my lifestyle and food preferences, being vegan would create more stress and difficulty in my life than the benefits of its healing nature, so I did not go to that extreme. I have friends for whom the vegan diet fits their lifestyle and nourishes them, but I knew it would not serve me in the same way. I also learned through mindfulness that awareness and clarity of mind keep me living as my best self, so I stopped consuming any sort of mind altering substances—yes, that includes caffeine. This has proven to keep me balanced in mind, body, and spirit, and helps me to intentionally show up for myself and the world. I try to eat as locally as I can to limit the global impact of shipping and support my local farmers. I don't put too much pressure on myself to prioritize this diet over connection, ease of lifestyle, and the occasional heart warming treat. Consuming in this way creates a healthy relationship between me and my body, and keeps me living as my best self. For this reason, I do not have to work hard to maintain the diet. It comes naturally and feels effortless.

Our ability to digest and absorb nutrients has a lot to do with who we are being while we eat. Seventy-five percent of our digestive efficiency is based on our attitude towards food and the state we are in while eating. If we are eating in a stress state or view food as the enemy, then we will be unable to absorb the nutrients and positive energy from our food. It is helpful to eat in a state of gratitude, recognizing the gift that was provided to you by the earth and all of the people involved in the preparations. We eat our food with the intention to use the energy it gives us to show up as the best version of ourselves.

You can use the following exercises to observe how your diet and relationship to food is affecting your mind, body, and spirit.

3.9.2 EXERCISES ON NOTICING HOW YOU CONSUME FOOD AND DRINK

Noticing what I eat and how it nourishes me

You can begin with a breathing and centering exercise. Follow the breath back into the body and mind. Connect with your physical form and open to listening to it.

Become the observer of your own diet.

Notice what you eat during the day. Notice what you drink during the day. For each item ask your body how it makes you feel.

How does it feel while you're eating it?

How does it feel while it's being digested?

How does it feel after it has been digested?

What does it do to your energy levels?

What does it do to your physical state?

What does it do to your mental state?

What does it do to the state of your spirit?

Does it contribute to your health, balance, and well-being or is it causing harm?

Repeat these questions for all of the things you eat and drink throughout the day. Ask your body what it would prefer to eat. What types of food and drink would most benefit your mental, physical, and spiritual well-being? Do the foods you eat contribute to you being the person you want to be?

Relating to food with gratitude

You will need a piece of fruit and your favorite snack for this exercise. You can begin with a breathing and centering exercise. Begin by holding your fruit in your hand with your eyes closed.

Examine the fruit as though experiencing it for the very first time. Feel the weight of the fruit in your hand. Touch the fruit becoming aware of its texture, its shape, its temperature, its every curve and wrinkle.

Now hold the fruit up to your nose and explore the smell of it. Try to find all of the different layers and nuances to the smell.

Now open your eyes and observe the fruit. Take in its every

detail. Examine all the different shades of its color. Notice its shape, its every wrinkle and fold, its every indent and bulge.

As you look at your fruit, become aware of all of the different elements contained within it. Notice that it is not separate from the rain that waters it, the air that gives it life, the sun that gives it energy, the soil that gives it nutrients. Notice every element that is within the fruit.

Remember that the fruit cannot exist without the plant or tree that grows it; without the roots, the stem, the leaves, and the flowers. Notice all of the energy that goes into producing the fruit. To prepare the earth, plant, cultivate, harvest, process, and transport. Imagine all of the people involved in the process. Imagine all of the energy spent to transport it, package it, place it on the shelves in your store, and sell it.

Look at all of these contributors with gratitude. Thank them all for providing you with this nourishment.

With this in mind, take a bite of your fruit. At first just allow it to sit in your mouth. Notice what your mouth and body does to prepare for consumption. The increase in saliva, the opening of the throat, the stomach coming alive. Notice how your mouth feels as it receives the food.

As you take your first bite, notice the burst of flavor. Chew slowly, recognizing how the taste and texture changes with each chew. Chew it until it is almost dissolved, and then swallow. Follow the bite all the way down the throat and into the stomach.

Receive the nourishment with gratitude. Set an intention for how you will use the energy provided to you and share it back out into the world.

You can repeat this same exercise with your favorite snack. Notice how much more is involved in the processing. Recognize that if the energy input to create the food is much higher that you will need to offer more energy back into the world after consuming it. Notice how consuming with this much awareness changes how and what you put into your body.

We don't only consume by ingesting. We are constantly consuming the sense impressions present in our environment. Our bodies receive 11 billion pieces of information from our environment at any one moment. The information our body receives turns into messages that are sent to our brain, becoming our perceptions of the world around us, which in turn produce our reactions. If we are constantly surrounded by overstimulating, toxic, or negative environments, then we will absorb them and take on the negativity within us. It will show up in our mental and physical health and in the way that we interact with the world and others. By becoming aware of what we absorb from our environment, we can make conscious choices on how to surround ourselves with things that promote our well-being and help us to show up as the person we want to be.

Our nose has a direct pathway to the brain-triggering memories, responses, and even altering brain matter. It has been found that both small and large molecules can pass from the nose into the brain and brainstem via the olfactory nerves.[13] This helps explain why diesel and black carbon breathed through the nose have been found to create lesions in the brain, increasing risk of autism, stroke, and cognitive decline. It has also been found that the scents of the forest called phytoncides lower blood pressure, act as an antiviral, and increase T cells in women with breast cancer.[39]

What we see is processed by the eyes and sent in messages to the thalamus and then the primary visual cortex in the back of the brain, where it is spread into three different processing systems. The more complex and busy our surroundings, the more work our brain has to do to process the information. Individuals living in cities with high levels of light pollution feel more stressed and have higher anxiety.[7] Nature landscapes that entice our attention but don't demand it allow our brain to recover from cognitive performance and executive attention make us calmer and more creative.[39]

Our ears receive information from the cochlea and send signals through the auditory nerve to the auditory center of the brain in the temporal lobe. The auditory brain processes these signals in three main areas. The auditory cortex may at first cause a reflex in the form of a jump or a turn of the head. It will then process it into a sound that can be consciously perceived and relate it to sounds heard in the past leading to the appropriate response. The more consistently noisy our surroundings, the more work our brain is constantly doing to process and respond. Individuals exposed to long term environmental noise have a twofold higher prevalence of depression and anxiety.[7] In quiet environments, our mind can relax from the consistent cycle of reacting, processing, and responding, which allows room in the brain for direct experience of our surroundings.

Natural environments are like a spa day for our senses. When surrounded by inspiring landscapes, soothing bird calls, and scents of pine and earthy soil, we give our senses a chance to relax and heal. Even if we do not live in the middle of a forest, we can make conscious choices to give our senses a chance to heal by spending time in a park or taking a weekend trip to nature. By simply noticing all of the stimulus around us, we become aware of how hard our system works to constantly process, and allow ourselves the breaks necessary to recover.

You can use the following exercises to notice what you are absorbing from your environment and give yourself a sensory break.

3.9.3 EXERCISES ON NOTICING YOUR SENSORY ENVIRONMENT AND GIVING YOURSELF A SENSORY BREAK

Noticing what's in your environment

You can do this exercise at any point during your day. Take a pause wherever you are. Sit in stillness for a few moments.

Tune into your sense of hearing as you tune all of your other senses out. Notice all of the things that you are hearing in your environment. Try not to label them, tell a story about them, or judge them, just listen.

Then tune into your sense of smell. Notice everything that you are smelling in your environment. Repeat for your sense of touch and then open your eyes and repeat for your sense of sight.

Now notice the state of your mind and body.

How is the body reacting to all of these sense stimuli?

How is your mind reacting?

Are you able to be calm and balanced?

Is your environment affecting you positively or negatively?

What needs to change in order for you to feel calm and healthy?

You can repeat this for all of the locations that you spend most of your time.

A break for the senses

This exercise will require you to change your environment to eliminate some of the sensory input present. You can do this by going to a quiet place in a park, by taking a bath in a quiet room, by sitting in a quiet peaceful place.

When you have arrived in this environment, repeat the previous exercise. Once you have tuned into all of your senses, then turn your attention towards your breath.

Simply listen to and feel the sensations of breathing. Tune everything else out. Allow the world and your mind to go quiet as the only thing present for you becomes the breath. Allow all of your other senses to take a break as you sit in stillness just you and your breath.

Paying attention to what we are consuming from media becomes more and more important in a world that spends up to seven hours a day in front of a screen.[32] Studies have shown that a vast amount of human values, styles of thinking, and behavior patterns are gained from extensive modeling in the symbolic environment of mass media.[4] This in turn means that the more people's images of reality depend on media's symbolic environment, the greater its social impact.[3] Essentially, what we are seeing in the media is becoming who we are. This is why it is so important for us to decide what it is we want to consume in the media. It becomes our perspective of reality and who we are within that reality.

As we scroll through media messages, we should notice what they are doing to our minds and bodies. If they produce feelings and sensations that take us further away from who we want to be, then we should distance ourselves and find a way to approach the information in a healthier, more productive way. Messages that invoke fear, despair, division, jealousy, self-judgment and hatred are not serving you. In a study conducted on 153 university students, 90% said that they had a fright reaction to mass media. More than half of the sample had subsequent disturbances in sleeping or eating patterns. A substantial proportion reported avoiding or dreading the situation depicted in the program or movie and mental preoccupation with the stimulus.[10] What you absorb from the media changes who you are being in the world, so choose what you absorb with discernment. The fear invoked from media messages can infiltrate into your daily life and make you react in ways that create more damage than the actual threat being portrayed. You can inform yourself of what's going on in the world while choosing to engage with messages that encourage peace, love, acceptance, and unity. Hold your own space of peace amongst the chaos so that we can continue to cultivate the good even when surrounded by disturbing messages.

The unmindful consumption of media can leave us susceptible to propaganda and fear-inducing control tactics that create division and the dehumanization of others. Media can alter our own moral sanctions by portraying more acceptable or rewarding outcomes for previously assumed unacceptable behavior. Fear is often used to justify what would otherwise be considered inappropriate or immoral behavior. When the media presents justifications of immoral behavior with evidence of threats and suggested solutions, we are more likely to act against our moral code. It has been found that people will behave in ways they normally repudiate if a legitimate authority sanctions their conduct and accepts responsibility for its consequences.[28] When we are fed stories of the threats others pose to us, we begin to see those people as the inhuman other. We are then offered solutions that may include aggressive behavior on how to mitigate the threat posed justifying immoral behavior as a means to protect ourselves. We then are told that the authorities sanction this behavior, meaning that when we partake in immoral acts we don't have to claim the responsibility. We saw this in the Holocaust and with the Japanese American internment during WWII, and we see it now with Muslim populations in the US. This chain of events is what leads an entire nation into condoning hate, division, greed, and destruction under the pretense that it will protect our own.

Because much of the media is not censored, this propaganda can be started by anyone. A Pew Research Center study conducted just after the 2016 election found 64% of adults believe fake news stories cause a great deal of confusion, and 23% said they had shared fabricated political stories themselves —sometimes by mistake and sometimes intentionally.[31] This means that we have to be more mindful than ever about what information we consume on the internet. We try to recognize the motivating factors behind every message and decide whether or not that message encourages behavior aligned with our moral values. This does not mean that we only read things that fit into our current belief system, but that we watch the reactions the message creates within us and decide whether or not it helps us stay in a place of peace, acceptance, love, and understanding.

Because we now have ways to share direct information that is delivered independent of time and space, and free of the controls of institutional and monetary gatekeepers, we are less dependent on a mediated filter-down system of persuasion and enlightenment.[4] Social media platforms provide outlets for anyone to share their beliefs and stories, allowing us to hear different perspectives and viewpoints. But in order to take advantage of this remarkable gift, we have to mindfully reach out to communities of different backgrounds and beliefs striving for understanding. In a study done in 2016, it was found that out of 376 million Facebook users having interactions with over 900 news outlets, the majority of people tend to seek information that aligns with their own views.[35] It takes effort to engage with difference, but the better we understand the other, the better we understand ourselves leading to more peace and unity in the world.

You can use the following exercises to begin examining how the media is influencing your perspective of reality.

3.9.4 EXERCISES ON MEDIA AND PERSPECTIVE

Examining your media use

You can begin with a breathing and centering exercise. Reconnect with self in non-judgmental awareness. We are not here to condemn, solve, or fix, but simply to observe so that we can understand ourselves and the world better.

While staying very present with your mind and body, begin to examine the amount of time you spend on social media and other media sources daily. Scan through what media sources you have contact with. Observe the different messages you are engaging with. Look into the source of the information you are receiving.

Who is writing this?

What is their agenda?

How do they show up in the world?

Now look into your motivation for engaging with it.

Do you want to be informed?

Do you want to belong?

Do you want connection?

Are you simply curious?

Now look into what this media is doing to the state of your body and your mind.

How is it making your body feel?

Are you tightening?

Where is your energy going?

Does it relax you or make you stressed?

Now look into how it makes your mind feel.

Are you feeling at peace?

Are you feeling angry?

Are you jealous?

Are you trying to prove something?

Are you feeling fearful?

Are you feeling inspired?

Who are you being now that you have this information? Is this who you want to be?

Now look into how you see the world now that you have this information.

Is this the perspective you want to have?

Is this perspective helping or harming you?

Do you need to engage with this media?

How would you change if you weren't engaged?

How would your perspective of self and the world change if you weren't engaged?

Is this who you want to be?

You can repeat this exercise with all the various sources of media you are engaged with each day.

Engaging with difference through media

You can begin with a breathing and centering exercise. Reconnect with self in non-judgmental awareness. Begin to observe the sources of media that you engage with.

Notice who the authors are. What is their nationality, their race, their gender, their political position, their religion, or social views?

Are your media sources always of the same perspective as you?

Are you hearing the other side?

Are you hearing varying perspectives?

How do you feel when you engage with a media source that does not align with your own views?

Do you learn anything?

Do you engage with sources from different countries, religions, and demographics?

Reflect on how your choice of sources affects the information you receive.

Are you getting the whole picture?

Are you able to develop compassion and understanding for those with different perspectives from your own?

Take the perspective of someone who engages only with media sources of a different opinion.

Are they getting the whole picture?

Do you believe that they understand you and your perspective?

Do you trust that they can have compassion for you?

Imagine yourself opening up and engaging with media from many different sources. Grow your understanding of difference. Notice how your own opinion seems less and less concrete. Allow this to open your heart and grow your compassion for and acceptance of difference.

It is no longer a question of whether or not social media should be used, but rather how it should be used. In 2019, 72% of Americans were using some form of social media.[31] We may see changes in trends of which platforms are used and how people engage with those platforms, but it is not likely that social media use will decrease. So the important question is "how can we help social media serve us rather than harm us?" A study conducted at Harvard suggests that social media can be positive if we engage with it mindfully, avoiding emotional connections like FOMO (the fear of missing out), dependency for social connection, and envy of other lifestyles.[6] Being mindful of our social media usage means noticing when we are engaging in positive interactions within social media and when we are engaging in negative ones that trigger harmful mental states within us.

The identity created for ourselves and others on social media has the potential to reconstruct our perspective of reality. We may only portray the sides of ourselves that we want others to see, creating a false perspective. The danger lies in this virtual reality being confused with the real one. Co-construction theory suggests that adolescents help to create the content of digital communication that shapes their lives, and that there may be strong continuity between adolescents' offline and online lives.[36] If we begin to believe that what we post and see on social media is an accurate depiction of real life, then we begin to place too much importance on media content and not enough on real life experience. Consequently, our reality is constructed predominantly by social media. It is unhealthy when we depend on social media for our understanding of and connection to the world around us.

FOMO (the fear of missing out) is one result of an overdependence on social media; it is due to an unhealthy emotional investment in online content.[40] Experiencing FOMO with social media use is correlated with higher anxiety and mood-related symptoms in everyday life.[5] The more we believe that life is happening within social media, the stronger our urge to be present with it becomes. This creates an addiction, leading to individuals spending an unhealthy amount of time connected to the internet. This overuse is reflected in the Pew Research showing that 72% of Americans use Facebook daily.[32] Feeling that life is always happening online rather than in the real world creates an anxiety whenever we are disconnected from the internet. We spend our days thinking about how we can represent our lives on social media rather than engaging with our current experience. We are constantly plagued by the feeling that we are missing out on something greater and bigger happening in the virtual world, and this keeps us from being fully present in the moment.

    The amount of time we spend maintaining and building relationships on Facebook may be negatively affecting the quality of our interpersonal relationships. It has been found that the loneliness of college students increases the more time they spend on Facebook.[27] It has also been found that by limiting the amount of time spent on Facebook to ten minutes a day both loneliness and depression went down in a group of undergraduates.[22] Not only are our social media friendships not giving us a sense of connection they are also decreasing our emotional and social development. Tween girls who are heavy users of online social interaction feel less normal and derive fewer positive feelings from interacting with friends. They also get less sleep, which is associated with negative mood and irritability.[29] If not used with awareness, social media may make us less able to have positive interpersonal relationships in our daily lives. Social media can be a good place to connect with new people and stay in touch with those distant from us, but it remains important to prioritize real interpersonal relationships over virtual ones.

One of the threats of virtual social networks is that they distance us from the actual human characteristics of the people we are interacting with. The less human and present someone feels to us, the more likely we are to cause them harm with no accountability. Sending a harmful message virtually removes us from the responsibility of having to watch the effects on the person's face and in their body language. Not being present for the ramifications makes it a lot easier to do. Though the virtual perpetrator feels much less of the effect of his/her act, the receiver still feels the same amount of pain, fear, and hurt, if not more, given that it is visible to a larger population. Statistics from i-SAFE Foundation found that over half of adolescents and teens have been bullied online.[24] The more people doing the bullying, the less responsibility each individual feels. If people engage in harmful acts on social media that are backed by several others, they are less likely to hold themselves accountable for the consequences.[4] We must be mindful of how our actions on social media affect others. A comment that is meant to harm, dehumanize, or humiliate someone else should never be sent, no matter what the justification may be. Remember that small comments create big waves in the lives of others.

Social media can be used to encourage new behavior. As long as we are mindful about the nature of the behavior our social media consumption encourages, then it becomes a tool for growth and expansion. The models shown to us from friends or groups in social media have a tendency to become the attitudes, beliefs, and actions that we adopt.[4] We must be aware of what we allow into our social media space because it might just become who we are. Opening up to new mindsets and ideas may inspire creativity by weakening conventional mindsets.[21] It may also inspire us to act benevolently by volunteering our services or donating time and money to causes that we would otherwise be ignorant to. But depending on what we engage with, it also has the potential to inspire harmful attitudes and actions. If we choose to fill our social media time with messages of hate, division, aggression, and greed, then we may find ourselves mimicking those same behaviors. Be discerning about what you allow into your social media space; verify that it aligns with the person you want to be.

After observing how social media increased how much I compared myself to others and decreased my present moment awareness because I was taking a picture that was destined for my news feed, I deleted all social media for many years. The freedom I felt was amazing and it actually increased the quality of my relationships. Instead of just looking at a friend's news feed to see how they were doing, I would send them a text, a letter, or call them. This provided much more genuine information than an image on a screen. It also freed my time and mind space to be more present for the actual world around me. I am now reconnected to social media for my business, but I only log in once a week and I don't post anything about my personal life. This allows me to access the convenience of connection and shared information of social media without it disrupting my well-being and presence.

You can use the following exercises to recognize how you are engaging with social media.

3.9.5 EXERCISES ON SOCIAL MEDIA

Understanding my relationship to social media

You can begin with a breathing and centering exercise. Reconnect with self in non-judgmental awareness. Begin to explore the amount of time you spend engaged with social media each day.

How often are you connected?

Where do you connect?

What is happening in the world around you while you are connected?

How do you feel when you are connected?

Why are you connecting?

What are you looking for?

What is social media providing you?

What is your motivation when you post updates or messages?

Who are you trying to connect with?

Do you actually feel connected to them?

How do you feel while you are posting?

How do you feel when you receive a lot of feedback on your posts?

How do you feel when you don't receive feedback?

How do you feel when you are unable to connect?

Do you ever feel anxiety around social media?

Have you ever posted anything harmful or hurtful?

Did you see the reaction of the people you harmed?

How did it make you feel?

Do you know how it affected others?

Do you know how any of your posts affect others?

How much of your identity is contained in social media?

Is this who you want to be?

Remember your heart's truth. Who you want to be in the world, what you value most, what you want to be offering the world and receiving from it. Can you create media content that reflects this version of you? That creates more peace, compassion, and love in the world?

Now look into the posts that you are consuming on social media.

What messages are you receiving?

What images are you seeing?

What perspectives are you getting?

How do you feel when you read a message?

What does it make you want to do?

How does it make you feel about self and about the world?

How do you engage with life after consuming these messages?

Do they help you to live as the person you want to be?

Do they motivate and inspire you?

How does engaging with social media affect your relationship with life?

Return again to your heart's values. Can you choose to consume social media content that inspires the true you, that motivates you to cultivate more positive energies in the world? Can you avoid the content that makes you feel less than, judgmental, or divisive?

Imagine yourself engaging in social media in a way that nourishes you and cultivates more of the energies you want to experience. Notice how engaging in this way fills you with more peace, purpose, and happiness.

We also consume the energies and attitudes of the people who surround us. We have all felt the collective power of a group inspired and motivated by compassion, love, and understanding. I feel this every time I participate in a healing retreat. In practice centers, I am surrounded by individuals who are diligently practicing to maintain their own well-being so that they can then pass it forward to end the suffering of others. This energy grows in the collective and strengthens the depth of one's own practice. Thich Nhat Hanh explains the importance of collective consciousness, saying that "When we come together to practice mindfulness, concentration, compassion, we generate these wholesome energies collectively, and it's very nourishing and healing."[20] Coming together with people who share the same aspiration to heal our planet and one another helps us to feel supported in our practice and encourages us to continue growing the collective consciousness.

Humans tend to take on the beliefs, mindsets, and behaviors of those surrounding them. If we surround ourselves with individuals who are angry, hateful, and divisive, then we will absorb those attitudes and begin to behave accordingly. Conversely, by exemplification, our social milieu can also encourage us to behave altruistically, through volunteering, donating, and caring for others.[4] For this reason, we must be mindful of who we surround ourselves with, and try to frequent social circles that encourage positive behavior and mindsets. The more effective our well-intentioned groups become, the higher their aspirations, the greater their motivation, and the more resilient to adversity they become, resulting in higher performance of their mission.[4] Choosing to surround ourselves with healthy and inspirational people will keep us healthy and inspired.

Broadening our social milieus and increasing contact with difference is also important for our personal and collective growth. We are more likely to be open to learning new ideas and practices from brief contact with acquaintances than from intensive contact in the same circle of close contacts.[17] Being in touch with a wide range of social milieus increases our understanding and acceptance of others and increases our own access to helpful ideas and practices. We know that people who have many social ties are more likely to adopt innovations than those who have limited ties to others.[33] By reaching out to new social groups and expanding our social network, we are opening ourselves to new resources and perspectives that can help us have a deeper understanding of ourselves while adopting what's useful from others.

As we reach out and connect with new social groups, we must be discerning as to which ones align with our true intentions. Stay mindful of how the ideas and practices of those you connect with are changing who you are. We should maintain the integrity of our deepest values and morals no matter who we are surrounded by. We can adopt new ideas without leaving behind our heart's truth.

You can use the following exercises to begin exploring how your social groups are affecting your thoughts and behaviors.

3.9.6 EXERCISES ON SOCIAL GROUPS

Examining my social groups

You can begin with a breathing and centering exercise. Reconnect with self in non-judgmental awareness. You can do this exercise while you are with your friends or on your own by simply imagining your interactions with your friends.

Begin to explore the people you surround yourself with on a daily basis. Call forth the ones you feel closest to. Identify the mood and intentions of each person in the group.

Observe their words and their actions.

Are their words delivering messages of peace, inspiration, and healing?

Or are the filled with judgment, division, and complaining?

Are their actions kind and supportive to self, others, and the world?

Or are the aggressive, selfish, and harmful?

Notice the reactions created in others by their words and actions.

Do people feel at peace around them?

Do they feel inspired around them and comfortable being themselves?

Recognize what perspective of the world this person has.

Do they see the world positively—in an inspiring and hopeful way?

How do they see themselves?

Acknowledge the mindset being encouraged in you.

Do they encourage you to be positive and kind?

Or do they inspire you to be negative and condemning?

Now notice who you are when you are around them.

Are you your true self?

Do they support your deepest values and truths?

Do they inspire you to grow and thrive?

Do they help you to maintain your well-being?

Do they reflect the way you want to see yourself and the world?

Are you who you want to be while around them?

Recognize that we become who we surround ourselves with. Remember who you truly want to be, your true values. Imagine building a friend group that supports this true version of you. A friend group that inspires you to continue on your healing journey. Notice how this makes it so much easier for you to stay true to your heart and your intentions. Notice how it brings more peace into your life.

Learning from difference

You can begin with a breathing and centering exercise. Reconnect with yourself in non-judgmental awareness. Observe how often you surround yourself with people who think differently than you.

Notice how you feel when you are confronted with opinions different from your own.

Do you become uncomfortable?

Do you feel judged?

Do you feel like you have to defend your opinion and make them think like you so that you feel safer?

Recall a time when you learned something new from someone who thought differently than you. Who was this person? Where were they from? And of what beliefs were they?

Did you allow them to be truly themselves around you?

What did you like about their perspective or lifestyle?

Did you incorporate anything new into your own beliefs or actions?

Did this bring any new wisdom or insight into your life?

Did it make anything easier or more joyful?

Now examine what you offer to others when you are allowed to be your true self.

Do you think that others learn something from you?

What do you feel that you offer to people?

How do you feel that you inspire others?

How do you encourage them to cultivate their well-being?

Are you who you want to be no matter who you're with?

Imagine that we allow everyone to be their authentic self around us. Trusting that they carry their own wisdom and insights that we could learn from. Trusting that they have their own ways of encouraging self-care and well-being.

Notice that when you approach people in this way that you open yourself up to learn so much more about the world and to connect with so many more people in compassion and understanding. Feel the peace and acceptance this brings you.

Being mindful of our consumption also means paying attention to what we buy and what we throw away. We should purchase in a way that limits waste and promotes healthy sustainable living. Of all the raw materials we take from the Earth, about two-thirds become waste, or the equivalent of 67 billion tons.[26] As we begin to notice our planet suffering the consequences of overconsumption, we begin to explore ways to reduce our environmental impact.

Currently we only capture 9% of waste in recycling. Plastics are becoming more and more complicated to repurpose. Although some companies are investigating ways to use recycled plastic to build sustainable roads, buildings, and indoor growhouses, most plastics still end up in landfills or in our oceans. What we buy and use has to end up somewhere after we are done with it. Becoming aware of where that is and how it affects our planet can help us to consume in a way that produces less single-use material.

Fast fashion has made clothing a disposable item resulting in the production of clothing to increase by one fifth between 2000 and 2015. The world threw away over $450 billion worth of the clothes made.[26] We buy new clothes even when we have tagged ones still hanging in our closets. Our over consumption of clothing is a waste of materials and resources. We can do our part by consigning old clothes and buying used clothes. Before buying new clothes look through your closet to see if you could repurpose something you already own or spice it up by combining it with different accessories. When purchasing new clothes, buy high quality ones that last for much longer and repair them when possible. We can create a lot less waste by taking care of what we already have and using it as long as possible before we throw it away.

The over-abundance of food has created a wasteful mentality.

One trillion dollars worth of food is wasted every year. This is the equivalent of one in every three grocery bags.[26] This is an insult to the earth and to every hand that went into producing edible food for humanity. You can do your part by buying only what you need. Shop more often, but buy less so that you can use all of the food before it goes bad. Make grocery lists with only the ingredients you will use for the weekly menu so that you aren't buying unnecessary items. Cook wilted vegetables into a stew instead of throwing them away. Pay attention to what you throw away and adjust your grocery list accordingly.

This is only the tip of the iceberg of the amount of products wasted and piled into landfills. Each one of us can participate in the movement by becoming mindful of what and how we are consuming.

The following exercises can help you to become aware of what you are consuming and wasting.

3.9.7 EXERCISES ON BECOMING AWARE OF MATERIAL CONSUMPTION

Becoming aware your material consumption

Before purchasing an item, pause, breathe, and assess why you are purchasing it. Do you really need it? How long will you keep it? What purpose will it serve in your life?

Before you purchase an item, take the time to recognize how much energy went into producing it. Notice what materials were used, who made it, how far it had to travel, and what it's packaged in. Consider if the energy and resources put into it are really worth consuming.

Before you purchase an item, notice how you feel. Are you purchasing this because you really need it, or because buying it meets another need in you? Can you nurture that need another way?

Observe the belongings that you have already. Do they all serve a purpose? Do you use them frequently? Do you have several that serve the same purpose? If you have more than is necessary, consider clearing the clutter by donating some of your belongings to those in need.

Before you throw something out, become aware of where that item will end up and how long it will be there. Is there another way to dispose of it that is more ecological? Can you recycle, repurpose, or donate?

Everything that we consume affects who we are and how we show up for others. By becoming mindful consumers, we can maintain our inner peace and cultivate well-being for ourselves and the world.

PART 4

Reaching Out
In Love

When our own peace and well-being is sturdy enough, we can begin to reach out towards others in love. This is truly the heart of our practice. We heal ourselves so that we can heal the world. The two go hand in hand because our well-being is interdependent with the well-being of the whole world. Doing our little part to help end the suffering of others is the beautiful fruit of our practice.

10

Continued Self-Love

Once we reach out towards others, it does not mean that our own inner work is done. We continue both simultaneously. We must always come back home to our own practice so that we are able to remain a positive presence for others. Our continued self-love is an act of love for others. As we have seen in the previous sections without understanding and compassion for self, there cannot be understanding and compassion for others.

If we have not found our own sources of happiness and grounding, we set unrealistic expectations for others hoping that they will solve all of our doubts, suffering, and insecurity. We expect their love will save us, make us whole, and give meaning to our lives. This is a very heavy burden for someone to carry, and they will most likely fall short, leaving us feeling bitter and angry.

In order to remove this burden from our loved ones, we

must understand how to find our own wholeness, safety, and purpose from within. Humans are flawed beings and are not capable of offering us everything that we need to be happy and healthy. That is why we have a practice that helps us identify all of the sources of happiness and health in and around us. Then we do not have to rely on one individual for all of our needs.

By continuing our practice and taking care of our own needs, we give ourselves the opportunity to connect with others free of unreasonable expectations. We can see them for who they are rather than for who we need or want them to be. We can offer them the freedom to pursue their own happiness and health instead of asking them to give us ours. This creates the opportunity for genuine connection and true love.

4.10.1 EXERCISES ON FINDING THE SOURCES OF OUR HEALTH AND HAPPINESS

What are my expectations

You can begin with a breathing and centering exercise. Reconnect with self in non-judgmental awareness. Explore your closest relationships or your partnership.

Be honest with yourself and identify what your expectations for these relationships are.

What are you hoping to get out of them?

Are you looking for security?

Are you looking for reassurance?

Are you looking for a sense of belonging?

Are you looking for approval?

Are you looking for a sense of purpose?

Can one person really give you all of these things?

Notice what your expectations are doing to the other person.

Are your expectations too heavy for one flawed human to carry?

Are you putting them up on a pedestal and expecting them to live up to it?

Are you able to be fully present for your loved one seeing and understanding who they really are?

Does your loved one feel comfortable being their true self around you?

Are you able to accept and love your loved one just as they are or is your love conditional on them doing or being what you want?

Are you setting yourself up for disappointment?

How are your expectations changing the way you relate to your loved one? Are you able to see them for who they really are and give them the opportunity to pursue their own happiness and well-being?

How do these expectations affect how you relate to others?

How do they affect how you show up for others?

Is this who you want to be?

My true sources of well-being

You can begin with a breathing and centering exercise. Reconnect with self in non-judgmental awareness. Examine what unrealistic expectations you have had for other humans.

What were they?

What do you feel like you are lacking that they can provide?

What holes are you expecting them to fill?

Now come back to your own heart space. Grow your heart space wider and larger with each breath. Notice that the heart space contains energies that are so much bigger than just you and that when you are connected in with them, you can receive all of the support and love that you need. Allow this to remind you of your own personal power to generate a sense of belonging, love, value, and safety from within.

When you are connected with your own heart space and your own personal power, what sources of these needs can you identify within and around you? What are the true sources of your wholeness and happiness?

What makes you feel grounded and stable?

When you are connected with these sources, how do you see yourself and the other?

Notice that you no longer see yourself as lacking and like you have take what you need from others. You no longer feel those empty spaces within you that others need to fill.

How do you relate to the others now that it is not out of need?

What are you able to offer the other?

What are you hoping to receive from the other now?

Notice that when you are not fixated on what you think you need to receive that you are able to accept what is being given. You can see that the world and others are giving you everything that you need in the form that they are able. You are able to open your heart and receive all the conditions of happiness that are present.

How do you show up for the people around you now?

Is this who you want to be?

Through our practice of self-love and understanding, we find wholeness and happiness from within, and this frees us to connect with others not out of need but out of love.

11

Mindful Communication

In order to reach out in love, we must practice mindful communication. I truly believe that the source of most conflict is a lack of understanding rooted in the inability to communicate effectively. We aren't listening to one another. We aren't expressing our true hearts to one another. We are speaking through layers and layers of hurt and wrong perceptions, weaving stories that dance around the essence of what we truly want and need to say. When we listen, we hear only the surface layers of people's stories, never diving into the heart of their message. When we react to something someone has said, we are reacting to their hurt, not to their heart. If we were really communicating on the level of the heart, we would see that there is not much difference between what we are all trying to say and what we all believe needs to be heard.

The first step to mindful communication is listening to self.

This is what we worked on in the first three sections of this book. If we are unable to hear our own needs and nurture them, then we will be unavailable to hear the needs of others. We will be trying so hard to be heard that it will over power our ability to listen. We see this all the time when two people talking don't even hear each other because they are so focused on trying to be heard. They are two people talking at each other while all the words simply hit the unreceptive wall and get lost into space, unheard by anyone. In order to truly listen to someone else, we have to be free of our own need to be heard, not forever, just for the moments of time that we dedicate to listening.

Before we try to listen to someone else, we check in with our own state of being. We examine if we have been listening to ourselves and if we have been giving ourselves enough self-love to be ready to listen to others. We can begin by coming back home to the breath and pausing to look inward. We recognize the state of our body and mind. We identify our own hurts and needs that may hinder our ability to fully see and hear the other. We become aware of the emotions within us that may change how we receive the message of the other. Even the greatest of practitioners will never be completely void of all of these self-centered preoccupations. Our goal is not to get rid of them, but to be aware of them. We notice when our ability to listen is hindered by our own preoccupations, creating unhelpful reactions and bring ourselves back to an open hearted awareness founded in love and compassion for the other.

We can then look into our perceptions and past experiences that may influence our ability to listen openly. What are we believing about the situation or the other person? What agenda do we have? Are we judging the situation from our own beliefs? These biased perspectives will get in the way of us being able to truly see the other. We are not trying to impose our own reality onto their story. We are trying to hear the heart of their reality.

You can use the following exercises to prepare for mindful communication.

4.11.1 EXERCISES ON UNDERSTANDING OUR OWN STATE OF BEING SO THAT WE CAN BETTER LISTEN TO ANOTHER

Examining your state of being

You can begin with a breathing and centering exercise. Come back home to the body, mind, and spirit. Rest in a state of non-judgmental awareness as you examine what you are experiencing in the body.

What sensations are present for you today?

How are you relating to those sensations? What stories are you telling about your physical state?

What reactions are the sensations creating?

How is this affecting your interactions with others and the world around you?

How will this affect your ability to listen openly?

Now switch your attention to your mind space.

What is present in your mind today?

What thoughts are loudest?

What is your current perception of self, other, and the world? What reaction are these thoughts and perceptions creating?

What emotions are behind these reactions?

How is this affecting your interactions with others and the world around you?

How will this affect your ability to listen openly?

Now switch your attention to the state of your spirit.

What is present in your spiritual being today?

Are you feeling grounded and supported?

Do you feel connected to your heart's truth?

How is this affecting your communication with others and the world around you?

How will this affect your ability to listen openly?

Acknowledge all of these conditions within you that may affect the way you show up for someone else. Know that they will influence your ability to listen and speak openly and lovingly. Be prepared to look beyond your own state of being to see into the state of the other.

Noticing the lens through which we listen to others

You can begin with a breathing and centering exercise. Come back home to the body, mind, and spirit. Rest in a state of non-judgmental awareness as you begin to explore your own ideas and perceptions on the situation of another. Listen to what they are saying about their experience—how they are relating to it, how they are feeling, what reactions they are having, what they believe they need to do to move through it.

Notice what is going on in your own body as you are listening. Are you feeling a resistance or a tightening? Notice what is going on in your mind. Do you feel like you need to fix or solve? What thoughts are you having about their experience?

Have you had similar experiences to this person that may change how you see their situation?

How did you relate to your experience?

How did you handle it? What judgments do you have about how others should handle it? How do you see the other person?

What ideas do you have about who they are and their place within the situation?

What opinions do you have about who they should be?

What emotions did you have around the experience?

Do you believe the other person will have the same emotions?

How did you respond to those emotions?

Are you predicting how the other person will respond or judging on how they should respond?

What was the outcome when you experienced a similar situation? What was your perception of the outcome?

Do you believe the other person should experience a similar outcome or a different one?

Are you predicting or projecting what their outcome should be?

After noticing all the ways that your own experience influences how you see and relate to the experience of the other, see if you can expand beyond your own experience.

Open your perspective beyond self, clearing your mind of all preconceived ideas and notions. Notice that the other person has their own ideas and perceptions and their own way of experiencing and relating to their situation.

Set an intention to listen in order to better understand their experience, and not project your own experience onto them. Listen to see the world through their eyes and help them find their way back to their own truth.

Once we have understood our own limitations to listening openly and set intentions to move beyond them, we can begin deep listening. Deep listening is a practice that needs consistent watering. It is not something that is learned once, mastered, and then perfected. It will continue to evolve and change as we evolve and change. We will continue to face different blocks and hurdles to deep listening depending on what we are experiencing in life at any given time. This is why we must always begin with the previous step of becoming aware of our state of being so that we know what obstacles we are facing and how to work with them. The obstacles will always be changing just as our state of being is always changing.

Deep listening involves listening without interjecting our own ideas and perceptions into what is being said by the other. We become void of our own needs and opinions so that we can fully hear and understand the needs of the other. We listen in order to know the other person better.

We can begin by noticing how we are seeing the other person. If we are seeing them as someone beneath us who needs our assistance, then we will be unable to listen with compassion. Deep listening requires a trust in the other person. We have to trust that they have all of the answers that they need within their own being. We have to believe that they are of divine nature just as we are. Thich Nhat Hanh explains that when the Vietnamese bow to one another, they bow to the Buddha nature within the other person. They see the other person as a spiritual being capable of reaching enlightenment. It is a sign of acknowledgment to the divine nature within all of us. When you listen deeply, you listen for the divine nature within the other person. You listen through all of the hurt and misunderstanding to hear the words of God within them. You trust that they are exactly where they need to be and that they are experiencing exactly what they need to experience in order to walk their own journey towards awakening.

Ralph Waldo Emerson said that he sees everyone as superior to him in some way and in that way he learns from them.[14] So he trusts that he can learn something from everyone. Every time we listen to someone, we open to hearing the wisdom that they carry within them. We are not trying to impart our own wisdom upon them. We are trying to listen so well that we can help the other person hear their own heart's truth.

Oftentimes when we listen to others, we begin to feel burdened and heavy with their suffering. This is because we take on their suffering as our own. We want to listen deeply to understand their suffering without making it our own. It is good to be able to relate to the person's story and to understand what they are going through, but it is not helpful to drop into the same state of being. We want to be able to understand their experience while maintaining our own well-being. It is helpful to remember that this person is on their own journey of healing and that they are experiencing exactly what they need to in order to rise above their own barriers. It is not up to us to fix them or to find solutions to their problems. We are listening in order to allow them to express their true heart and find their way to their own answers. This relieves us of any pressure to resolve their problems or get too enmeshed in their suffering.

While you listen try to hear the true essence of what the

other person is saying. This is what lies under the surface layer story. The essence is what they are feeling within and how the core of their being has been affected by the experience. Listen for the true message under the hurt, blame, and desire. What is the heart really asking for? We can get in touch with this by noticing what is being said under their words. This is found in their eyes, their body language, their facial expressions, and their physical energy. By reading their body, we can get closer to their true feelings. Remember how your body informed you about your internal state and use the same clues to tune into their internal state. They may feel something very different from what their words are indicating and their body will alert you to it. If we get wrapped up in just their words, we may get thrown off track from what their heart really needs.

Never tell the person that they are wrong or try to correct them or change their perspective. This will stop the progress of their healing. Simply allow them to speak until they can hear their own heart. Oftentimes, it can take a lot of words based on misunderstanding before we can hear our own truth. As we speak uninterrupted, we often catch our own mistakes and recognize our own misperceptions. By the time we are done, we may have solved our own problem without any advice or input from the other person. The listener's job is simply to encourage free and open expression.

Be very aware of your state of being through the whole process of listening. If you find it too difficult to listen deeply, then tell the person you need some space to take care of yourself before coming back to listening. Our society has made us afraid of silence and of disengaging from conversation. We believe that it is rude to walk away and ask for space. This does us much harm. If we don't walk away when we are no longer able to listen with compassion, then we will be adding to our own hurt and the hurt of the other. It is better to find peace in silence than to build hate, animosity, fear, and anger in conversation. Respect your state of being and recognize your ability to listen with compassion so that each conversation you have generates more understanding and peace.

4.11.2 EXERCISES ON DEEP LISTENING

Seeing the divine nature of the other

You can begin with a breathing and centering exercise. Once you are reconnected with self, you can bring your focus back to your heart space where love, compassion, peace, and acceptance reside. From the eyes of the heart look deeply into the person you would like to listen to.

How are you seeing them?

Who do you believe they are?

What do you believe they are capable of?

Can you see them as a divine being capable of finding all the wisdom they need from within?

Do you believe they possess knowledge that could teach you something? Do you believe that you will gain greatly from the opportunity to listen to them?

Look into their eyes and see their beauty.

Trust that they are on the exact journey that they need to be on in order to awaken.

Trust that they are on their way towards healing.

Trust that their experience is exactly what is needed on their journey towards awakening.

Can you offer them the freedom to go through this experience in their own way?

Can you offer them love and acceptance even if they are doing things differently than you would?

Can you support them even if they do not think like you?

Notice how this allows you to be present for them in love and acceptance and how this type of deep listening facilitates their exploration of their own heart's truth. Allow this to bring a peace to both of you.

Listening to the heart

You can begin with a breathing and centering exercise. Once you are reconnected with self, you can bring your focus back to your heart space where love, compassion, peace, acceptance, and gratitude reside. Imagine an opportunity you have had to listen to another.

Listen to the words that they are saying. Hear the story that they are telling. Hear the misperceptions, anger, blame, fear, and judgment.

Now listen below the story. Look into their eyes and into their heart. Notice what their body language is telling you. Notice their breathing and their facial expressions. Notice what their hands are doing and the tension in their body.

What are they really trying to say?

What is their heart asking for?

What hurts are at the root of what they are saying?

What needs healing?

Where is peace needed?

How are they perceiving themselves?

How are they perceiving others and the world?

What are their words really trying to achieve?

What can you learn from their words?

What wisdom is beneath their story?

What growth can come from this experience?

Notice that when you are listening instead of trying to convince, solve, or fix that you can hear truths in their words that give you insights into your own experiences. You can begin to understand the deeper meaning to their experience which helps you to understand the deeper meaning within your own.

Notice how in deep listening we allow the other person to find their way to their own wisdom and their own growth. If you respond to anything in what they say, respond to this. Point out their wisdom and their growth helping them to move towards healing.

As we listen to the heart of what the other person is saying our only desire is to understand the other person better so that we can help them to suffer less. We can begin by asking them if they feel that we understand them well enough. We can express our desire to understand them better. As we listen, we engage in ways that reflect what we have heard and then we ask for clarification when necessary. Begin by restating what the other person has said, starting with, "What I hear you saying is_____." Try to stay as accurate to their own words as possible. Hearing what we have said repeated back to us helps us to understand ourselves better and reach the truth of what we are trying to say.

We try not to feed the negativity of the other person by agreeing with judgmental or accusatory statements that they make. At the same time, we do not try to correct them or negate what they are saying. We do not add onto their story, give our perspective, or offer advice. We simply listen quietly, not agreeing or disagreeing, just reflecting exactly what it is that they are saying to us.

Once the person has expressed themselves fully, we can ask clarifying questions. This is a delicate task because we do not want our questions to lead them towards any certain answer. It is helpful to recall what we discovered in our own state of being so that we aren't trying to impose our own views or perceived solutions on the other person. Our questions should remain void of our own opinions. We can ask things like: What do you mean by _____?, Can you explain _____ more?, What do you feel when _____?, What does _____ mean to you?, How do you interpret _____?, Tell me more about _____. These conversational prompts simply lead the speaker to explore their own ideas and perceptions further.

Often as the other person is going in depth to explain their point of view to you, they begin to discover their own misunderstandings and the role they played in the situation. As they talk themselves through their own resolution process, they find their own solutions. Even if they do not arrive where we believe they should, we can trust they received some clarification simply by talking their way to understanding themselves better.

The whole time we are listening, we see through the eyes of compassion. We trust that the other person knows their life and their experience better than we do and that they will arrive at a resolution that is best for them. Our only desire is to help them suffer less, not to judge them, condemn them, or change them.

The only time that we should give input is if we are asked. If they do ask for our input we are careful to give a reflection on what they are saying, not our perspective on the situation. We can do this by saying things like: You said that you are feeling_____ because _____, You said that _____is not helpful and that you would rather _____, You said that _____ really affects you negatively and that you want to move more towards _____. You can always conclude by asking if that feels true to them. We are simply using their own words to highlight some aspects of their experience and clarify their situation.

If it seems helpful and appropriate, we can use examples from our own lives to give encouragement or show empathy. We share our own experience without projecting it onto the other person or expecting that they should react similarly. We can do this by saying things like: When I experienced _____ I found it helpful to _____., When I went through _____I used _____ to help me. We share a similar experience, how it affected us, and what we did to heal from it. Remind them that this is what worked for you and how you experienced it, but that it can be different for everyone.

Once they are finished sharing, show empathy for their situation without feeding into any self-sabotaging beliefs or victim mentality. Remind them of their strengths and of their own wisdom. Connect them with the solutions they themselves arrived at.

4.11.3 EXERCISES ON COMPASSIONATE UNDERSTANDING

Listening in order to hear, understand, and show compassion

Practice deep listening with a friend. It may be helpful to tell them what you are doing.

Invite them to share an experience that has been troubling them lately. Listen with compassion.

Don't agree or disagree.

Don't feed their story.

Don't correct, fix, or judge.

Just listen.

Then show them what you heard by repeating it back to them. Ask clarifying questions.

If they ask for advice, share a similar experience you have had. Show empathy for their situation. Remind them of the solutions they found within and connect them back to their own wisdom.

When we speak, our motivation should always be to heal self and the world. Our words should come from a place of openness, understanding, compassion, and reconciliation. Thich Nhat Hanh explains that Right Speech has four main qualities. It has to be the truth, it should not be an exaggeration, it should be consistent, and it should be peaceful.[18] These seem like very simple guidelines to follow, but most of us break every single one on a daily basis. In order to generate right speech, we have to be very self-aware and have a deep understanding of what we are truly experiencing. We cannot speak our truth if we do not know what it is. We cannot be accurate if we don't hold accurate insights. We cannot be consistent if we are not internally sound and stable. We cannot speak peacefully if we do not have peace within. The art of right speech is developed through a deep understanding of self.

An understanding of self requires a consistent mindful practice of looking inward and observing. We must consistently practice all of the mindful techniques taught in the previous chapters of this book. To be honest with others we have to first be honest with ourselves. We have to know what we feel and experience in order to convey it accurately to others. Otherwise we will be sharing information that is not our own; experiences have been relayed to us by others of which we have no direct knowledge.

Speaking the truth means only relaying information that we have direct knowledge of or sharing our own experiences. Speaking truth does not mean that we share our own beliefs and opinions as though they were an ultimate truth. As Parker Palmer explains so well in his book *A Hidden Wholeness*, "Truth does not favor those who believe that there are absolute answers to the deepest questions and that those who know the answers are obliged to convert everyone else."[30] We do not speak to convince, solve, fix, or change others. We speak to share our own personal experience in hopes that it will add a layer of insight to the collective understanding of truth. We share "our truth," which is what we have personally experienced and how we personally view a situation, understanding that this may differ from how others view the same experience. We simply add one more perspective to fill in the "greater truth," which (unless we develop a deep understanding of every perspective on the planet) will never be "our truth." This is the difference between "our truth" and the "greater truth." The "greater truth" is compiled of the inner wisdom and perspective of every being on the planet and we as individuals will never possess it. All that we can speak on is "our truth," and in order to speak "our truth," we "speak about our life and vulnerability, not opinions, ideas, and beliefs."[30]

    The biggest hindrance to sharing our truth with others lies in not being honest about it to ourselves. Oftentimes, our heart knows truths that our mind is unwilling to acknowledge. There may be layers of shame, denial, or fear that keep us from hearing our own truth. Having a consistent mindfulness practice helps us to make peace with whatever it is that we are experiencing and to be honest with ourselves about it. There is nothing too big or too dark to be held within our heart space. When we trust that we are a part of something much greater than us, and that our personal journey is exactly what it needs to be in order for us to live our purpose, then we accept every experience in our life as a crucial stepping stone towards our evolution and healing. Nothing does not belong. Nothing is shameful or embarrassing. Everything that we live and experience is exactly as it should be, and sharing it honestly with ourselves and others allows it the exposure to love that it needs in order to transform and heal.

4.11.4 EXERCISES ON FINDING YOUR TRUTH

Finding your truth

You can begin with a breathing and centering exercise. Reconnect with your inner self and open to listening and receiving what you hear. Breathe out all of your opinions, beliefs, and judgments. Breathe out any labels or confining identities that define you and your thoughts.

Open your mind to simply experiencing without fixing, solving, or controlling. Just be with your internal experience.

Explore what you are feeling in your body without explaining it with beliefs or opinions without trying to fix it or solve it.

Explore what you are feeling in your mental space without explaining it with beliefs or opinions without trying to fix it or solve it.

Explore what you are experiencing in your spirit and heart space without explaining it with beliefs or opinions, without trying to fix it or solve it.

How would you share what you are experiencing with someone else without using your beliefs, opinions, or ideas?

Simply share your experience and vulnerability without having to explain it, solve it, fix it, or convince anyone else of its validity.

This is your truth.

Uncovering hidden truths

You can begin with a breathing and centering exercise. Reconnect with your heart space, this space of nothing but love, compassion, peace, and acceptance. Know that this space can hold all things while nurturing and loving them.

Look with the eyes of your heart space at your life. Know that everything you live and experience belongs. Know that your journey is exactly what it needs to be in order for you to live your purpose. Trust that all experiences in your life can be used to heal you and to heal others.

With this deep knowing look again at your truth.

Is there anything that you have been unwilling to look at or admit?

Is there anything that you have kept hidden from yourself or others?

Call it back into your heart space and hold it tightly.

This too belongs.

This too is a part of your healing journey.

Imagine sharing this truth with yourself and the others in this sacred heart space. Picture the love of acknowledgment shining down on it.

Notice how this sad and dying seed needs the light, fresh air, and cleansing waters to be able to transform and grow into something beautiful.

Notice how when it is showered with love, it cannot hold any darkness. Notice how when it is embraced by compassion, it is given the opportunity to heal, and the healing it experiences through you can be used to heal all others.

Hold your truth in your heart and shine a light on it so that it can no longer hold the darkness.

How we share our truth is also very important. If we have truly grasped the concept of truth, then we will not exaggerate because an exaggeration is not the truth. We will be consistent because there will only be one version to our truth. Speaking peacefully is perhaps the hardest component of Thich Nhat

Hanh's Right Speech. Speaking peacefully means that we tell the truth in a way that leads to understanding and healing not to division, hurt, or blame. Before speaking, we should always ask ourselves, "Why am I telling them this and how will it affect them?" This will help clarify the intent of our words. Sometimes the truth may create initial suffering that will lead to deeper healing later. If this is the case, then we have to be sure to deliver the truth delicately while the other person feels safe and has access to all the tools necessary to help them through the difficulty. We also make sure to deliver the message with compassion. Even if our words have to be firm they can still be compassionate. Your aim is not to hurt the other person but to help them understand.

In order for our speech to increase understanding, we have to make sure we deliver it in a way that is comprehensible to the other person. We have to consider the other person's culture, background, and experiences so that we can speak to their knowledge. We use words and examples that are familiar to them. If I speak to a Christian, I may use words within their religion rather than words within mine. This does not mean that I change my truth, I simply word it in a way that can be heard by them. If I use terms of a belief system that is not theirs, they will have a harder time receiving what I say. Focus on the deepest content of what you are saying, not the verbiage used to say it. You can give the same message using a wide array of vocabulary.

The Buddha once described how he delivered messages by saying, "I have to speak according to the mind of the person who listens and the ability of that person to receive what I share."[18] Think about it the same way as the difference between how you explain a topic to a child versus a scholar. You may be telling the same truth to both of them, but they will need it to be delivered very differently in order to receive it. If you talk to the scholar like a child you will insult him and he will not listen to you. If you talk to the child like you would to the scholar, the child will not be able to understand what you are saying, and so will not receive it. We have to speak directly to our audience in a way that they can hear us. The essence of what we say will stay the same, but the delivery may change.

When we speak "our truth," we are doing our part to generate the "greater truth." We can tell "our truth" without discounting other truths or building divisions. Just because we see the world one way does not mean that there aren't other valid ways to see it. As Parker Palmer says, "If we want to live in the truth it is not enough to live in the conclusions of the moment. We must find a way to live in the continuing conversation with all its conflicts and complexities, while staying in close touch with our own inner teacher. We can dwell in the truth by dwelling in the conversation. Our differences are laid out clearly and respectfully alongside each other. We speak and hear diverse truths allowing us to grow together towards a larger, emergent truth that reveals how much we hold in common."[30]

Speak to deepen understanding and connection slowly, working towards a larger truth that includes all beings.

4.11.5 EXERCISES ON SPEAKING YOUR TRUTH

Sharing your truth in peace

You can begin with a breathing and centering exercise. Tune back into your heart space and listen deeply to what truth you may need to share with someone in your life. Examine why it is important for you to share this truth with them.

Will sharing it help you to heal as well as them?

What effect will sharing it have on the other person?

Is it a truth that is easy for them to hear?

How will it help them to heal?

Imagine yourself telling them this truth.

Where should you be so that they can feel safe while hearing it?

When should you tell them so that they have time to process and digest your message?

How should you deliver it so that the words are peaceful and compassionate, not full of anger and hate?

Feel the state of your own body that will help you to present the message in a peaceful way. Make sure that your body is relaxed and open to the other person.

Imagine yourself delivering your truth in this way.

How does the other person receive it?

Can they hear you?

What is the energy between you?

What is their reaction?

Did you maintain peace and compassion while delivering your truth?

What does this do to your connection with the other person?

Can you see that it deepens your connection when you feel safe sharing your truth? Notice how nice it feels not to have to hide who you truly are or what you are feeling or experiencing. Notice how the other person can develop compassion and understanding for you. Notice how they open to their heart to you when they feel that you trust them with your actual truth.

Sharing your truth with all

Once you have come in contact with your truth, imagine yourself sharing it to three different people. The first person would be a close friend who shares your culture, background, and many of your experiences.

What words would you choose and how would you present it?

The second person is a young child who is close to you.

What words would you choose and how would you present it?

The third person is someone of a different culture and belief system who does not share very many similar life experiences with you.

What words would you choose and how would you present it?

Are you staying true to the essence of the message in each of these deliveries?

This is your truth.

The hardest time to speak our truth is when it leaves us open and vulnerable to a loved one who has hurt us. Our first reaction to being hurt is usually to punish the other person so that they feel the pain that they caused us. This may appear in many forms. We may yell, fight, and blame. We may say other hurtful things to them unrelated to how they hurt us. We may turn away from them and give them the cold shoulder. All of these hurtful habits lead to further disconnect rather than healing, but we do them because we are afraid to show our vulnerability and ask for help.

Healing can only happen when we are honest with our experience of suffering. If we truly trust our partner and our ability to help one another to heal, then we have to tell the truth. Telling the truth does not mean blaming the other person for all of our suffering and rehashing everything they have done wrong. It means sharing our experience of the pain. It means sharing our own vulnerabilities and fears and asking them for help.

This process always starts by spending time looking inward to truly understand what it is you are feeling. After you have been triggered by a loved one, you can let them know and then ask for some time and space to explore the cause. Why were you really hurt by the situation? What basic needs felt threatened? We don't focus on what the other person did but rather on what feelings it brought up in us and the insecurities within us that caused them. This process was covered in the section on emotions. We uncover the root cause of our emotional distress within us that was triggered by the other person. Our negative emotions were not caused by the other person, only triggered by them. The other person cannot trigger us if there is no insecurity within us to be triggered. So we take responsibility for our own feelings and we uncover their root cause.

When I feel hurt by my partner or want to talk through something that has been troubling me, I don't speak to him right away. I spend days and sometimes weeks meditating on why his actions or the situation brought up those feelings in me. I identify which of my needs weren't being met. Once I identify those needs, I first look for my own resources for meeting them and examine if I had been neglecting self-care practices leading to a greater dependence on him to generate my well-being. Before telling him that he needs to do something to make me feel better, I engage in the self-care that will improve my own state of being. Once I am grounded and centered, I can speak to him from a calm and loving place motivated by the desire to increase our connection and intimacy rather than a desperate demand for him to make me feel better.

Once we know the root cause of our emotional distress, we prepare to share it with the other person. We use this time to understand each other better so we are not only sharing our own experience but deeply listening to the experience of the other. Always start by thanking the other person for their presence and willingness to listen. Acknowledge that you are happy that they are there. Tell them you are suffering and need their help. This seems silly, but it is so important. After we have been hurt by someone, it takes much humility and vulnerability to admit that we want them near us and that we need their help to heal. It is much easier to treat them like the enemy and push them away. The other person may even have a belief that you don't want them near you and they may be afraid to approach you. This reassures them that you do value their presence and that you trust them to be a part of the healing.

My partner had a fear of these conversations, because he saw them as a sign that things weren't going well in the relationship, which meant he was failing in some way. It took a lot of practice and explaining to help him recognize that being able to engage in these conversations was actually a sign of strength in the relationship. It meant that we were dedicated to understanding one another better and working through the hard moments so that we could become closer. Starting the conversations with a reminder about how much we care about each other and how we want to help one another heal and connect on a deeper level sets the tone for the conversation from one of blame and anger to one of love and compassion.

Once you set the tone for the conversation, you can share your own experience. Speak to that inner need that felt threatened. Speak directly to your vulnerability. Blame and anger are simply shields from our own vulnerability and will create higher walls between us and the other person. Don't tell them what they did wrong and how it's their fault. Tell them what hurts within you. For example: This triggered my fear of abandonment and I felt _____., This brought up my belief that I'm unlovable and I felt _____., This threatened my need for freedom and I felt _____. Then share what you really need. For example: I need to feel loved., I need to feel safe., I need to feel free and independent.

Once you have shared your true feelings, ask the other person to help you to understand them better. You can ask them to share their own experience and what needs they were experiencing or trying to fill for themselves. You can start by saying please help me to understand why you _____ and what you were feeling when you _____. This gives them the opportunity to express their truth to you. While they are sharing you are practicing deep listening. Don't try to correct them, point out their misunderstandings, or condemn them for their behavior. Just listen to understand. After they have fully expressed themselves and have heard how you experienced their actions, they may correct themselves without you having to do anything. Or you may come to realize that what they said or did was not a sign that they don't love you or value you, but was due to their own lack of understanding or their own unmet needs.

This gives both of you the opportunity to understand each other's needs better and find ways to nurture those needs together. You can ask one another what you can do to help meet their needs so that they don't feel hurt in the future. This does not mean that one person changes all of their behavior so that they never trigger the other person. It is helping each other to heal the inner unmet needs that lead to being triggered. For example: How can I help you to feel safe when your fear of abandonment has been triggered? How can I help you to feel independent when you feel your freedom has been threatened? How can I help you to feel loved when you feel unlovable? The other person is still responsible for taking care of their own feelings and needs, but we can help them in the process by reminding them that we do care and that we are here to love them and support them.

Always finish the conversation by reminding each other of how much you care about one another and how you are both doing your best to heal your own suffering so that you can both heal together. We have to continually work on healing ourselves so that we can show up intentionally for others. The healing process does not happen by asking one person to do all of the healing and growing alone. You have to heal and grow together. You can also remind one another that you have their best interest in mind and that your intentions toward them are always good, even if sometimes you make a mistake.

4.11.6 EXERCISES ON ASKING FOR HELP WHEN SOMEONE HAS TRIGGERED YOUR SUFFERING

Becoming aware of what I'm really feeling

Before you blame or attack the other person for triggering you, pause and come back home to self. Examine your own internal state and the root cause of your emotional distress. You may want to use the exercises in the section 2.4 to become aware of your emotions.

Asking for help in healing

Once you know the root cause of your emotional distress, follow these steps to ask for the other person's help to heal.

1. Ask them to have a conversation because you are suffering and you need their help to heal.

2. Remind them that you are grateful for their presence and that you are happy they are there.

3. Tell them what need in you felt threatened and what emotional response it brought up.

4. Tell them what you need in order to feel safe and loved.

5. Ask them to help you understand their words and actions better and listen deeply to their response.

6. Ask each other how you can support one another in your healing.

7. Remind each other that you are both doing your best to heal your own suffering so that you can heal together.

8. Remind each other that your intentions toward one another are always good and that you always try to prioritize each other's well-being.

Mindful communication is the foundation of loving relationships. If we do not know how to communicate effectively, then we are unable to connect with the people in our lives in a healthy and meaningful way. A failure to communicate is one of the leading reasons for failed relationships. We have to be able to share our truth with the ones we love so that we can live authentically together, helping one another to heal and grow. Only after we develop the capacity to communicate effectively can we begin to love genuinely.

12

Mindfully Loving Others

As with every mindful practice, loving others begins with your ability to love self. Whatever we are offering ourselves is what we will have available to offer others. If our hearts are filled with more compost than flowers, then compost is what we will offer others. In order to offer others flowers, we must first work our own internal gardens and cultivate them for ourselves. We will always have a combination of both compost and flowers, as one can never be present without the other. Being genuine means that we are honest with ourselves and others about our internal state. There will be times when we do not have much to give. In those moments, it is alright to admit it to the people in our lives and turn inward to offer ourselves some love. Loving others does not mean that we are always in perfect condition. It means that we are honest with where we are at and we make an effort to take care of ourselves so we can better take care of others. If we lie about how we are and try to help when our own internal state is out of balance, then we may be doing more harm than good.

Love yourself enough to be honest about what you need in order to be healthy and balanced. Recognize what needs to be nurtured within you and connect with the sources of that nurturing within yourself and the world around you. As Rumi says, "Your job is not to seek for love but merely to seek and find within yourself all the blocks and barriers against it. Embrace the barriers and bring kindness to them."[34] Notice what piles of compost darken your ability to love, and start turning them into nutritious soil. Water the good seeds within yourself and start growing your own heart's garden so that you have beautiful, luscious flowers to share with others.

4.12.1 LOVING SELF AND GROWING OUR OWN HEART'S GARDEN

Loving self

You can begin with a breathing and centering exercise. Follow your breath inward and reconnect with self. Notice the ways that you are taking care of yourself.

Are you allowing yourself enough time to turn inward and reflect?

Are you present enough with yourself to understand your internal state? Do you understand your own suffering enough to nurture yourself and heal?

Are you connecting with your own sources of happiness and joy?

Are you giving yourself the freedom to be your authentic self and not just following external expectations?

Are you listening to your needs and honoring them?

Are you accepting where you are and relating to your present experience in peace?

Are you loving yourself enough to love others?

Know that you are love and that love can hold all things.

Allow your love for self to grow and expand. Repeat to yourself; I love you, I love all of you, I am love, love is me.

Growing your heart's garden

You can begin with a breathing and centering exercise. Come back to yourself and focus on your heart space. Notice what is present in this space.

Is it open and free to love and accept?

Are there some things that are heavy on your heart preventing it from being open?

Be honest with the difficulty within you. Know that the heart space can hold, nurture, and heal all things. Trust that this too can be used for growth and healing.

Look into your compost and notice what needs to be nurtured and healed within it. Imagine yourself offering this nurturing to yourself and slowly turning the compost into workable soil. Imagine the sun and rain finally being able to reach the dark places you have been hiding.

Notice as the rain cleanses them and the sun brings them to life. Notice how as you work the compost that your good seeds can begin to grow. Imagine planting your seeds of peace, love, compassion, and acceptance.

Water them with all your good intentions. Watch as they grow into a beautiful field of flowers. Imagine the flowers in your heart's garden, their brilliant colors and sweet smells.

Now imagine offering these flowers to the people in your life. Share all of the beauty and love that you have cultivated with the people around you. Notice how it feels to have all of these beautiful flowers to share with others. Feel how your heart space has grown.

As we begin to turn our love outward, we focus on cultivating four main qualities to that love. Thich Nhat Hanh says that these four qualities are Compassion, Happiness, Joy, and Freedom.

The first quality is compassion. Compassion means that we truly want to understand the other person's suffering so that we can help them to heal. This does not mean that we take on their suffering and the responsibility of fixing them. It means that we are courageous enough to listen to and hear their suffering so that we can understand them better and help them to suffer less.

This is not an easy task and requires a great deal of stability within ourselves. Pema Chodron says that "The only reason we don't open our hearts and minds to other people is that they trigger confusion in us that we don't feel brave enough or sane enough to deal with. To the degree that we look clearly and compassionately at ourselves we feel confident and fearless about looking into someone else's eyes."[11] Only if we are able to look into our own suffering with compassion are we able to do so for another. If we have not understood our own suffering, we may feel triggered and destabilized when we hear the suffering of another. This would force us to turn away when someone is opening their heart to us because we are fearful that what they share will throw us off balance. Truly loving means that we are sturdy enough to stay present when the other opens their heart to us.

Whenever I am lacking compassion for others, it is because I have not been showing myself enough compassion. If I have been putting pressure on myself to push through pain and suffering to continue being productive, then I have no empathy for someone who is tired and in need of rest. If I have neglected my own difficult emotions, stuffing them down so that I can wear a smile for others, then I have no empathy for someone who is expressing sadness or grief. When I lose patience with others, it is probably because I have not been giving myself any grace in my own life. So, if I am struggling to offer compassion to the people in my life, I first look inward and examine how compassionate I am being with myself. Sometimes this means that I need some time and space for self-care before becoming present for others.

When we are ready to be present for others, we can go back and practice all of the techniques of deep listening in order to hear them better. We simply listen to understand their experience and to help them reach their own inner truth and healing not to force our own perspectives, needs, or solutions onto them. We can then remind them that we are here for them and that we love them no matter what they are struggling with. It is very difficult to be with someone in their suffering without needing to fix them. The need to fix comes from our own discomfort with suffering. We can't bear to see the other person suffer so we want to fix them right away. Compassion means that you can stay with them even in their suffering. Allow the suffering so that they may find their own clear and honest path out of it.

Compassion builds trust, the trust that you can accept and love one another even in your moments of pain and vulnerability. Give each other permission to be honest with your suffering without running from it or immediately trying to fix it. Love each other even though you struggle. Brene Brown says that "We cultivate love when we allow our most vulnerable and powerful selves to be deeply seen and known and when we honor the spiritual connection that grows from that offering with trust, respect, kindness, and affection."[8] In order for love to grow, we have to show our vulnerability and trust that the other person can hold it in respect, kindness, and affection. This is compassion. Create the space to allow the other person to suffer in your presence, with your only intention being to understand their experience better.

I grew up in a family that liked everyone to appear happy, so there wasn't much room for difficult emotions. This made me quite intolerant of negative emotions. If I ever had one, I felt like I had to fix it right away so that I could go back to being happy for everyone else. Treating myself this way made me treat others in exactly the same way. I was uncomfortable around them if they were sad or hurting, so I would go right into fix it mode. I would try to cheer them up or point out the silver lining. This did not help me or them to actually heal from the difficult experience, and made them avoid me when they were struggling. Once I gave myself permission to feel my emotions and be with them in love, I was able to heal from them instead of simply suppressing them. Becoming comfortable with my own emotions made it easier for me to be present for other people when they were experiencing difficult emotions. This developed deeper connections between me and my loved ones because they felt safe in my presence no matter what they were experiencing in their emotional world.

4.12.2 EXERCISES ON COMPASSION

Examining your own stability

You can begin with a breathing and centering exercise. Come

back home to self and ground in your heart space. Remember that you are love. Observe how stable and grounded you feel.

Are you able to look into your own suffering?

Look into your suffering.

Do you know what makes you suffer?

Have you been holding, nurturing, and healing your own suffering?

Do you trust that you have all the resources necessary to heal your suffering?

In trusting your own ability to stay grounded even in the presence of your suffering, do you feel stable enough to see the suffering of others?

Imagine yourself centered in your own heart space, knowing that you don't have to solve or fix. Know that your only role is to be present in love and compassion so that you can hear the suffering of another.

Are you stable enough to be present?

Can you trust in your own heart's ability to hold the suffering of another in peace, acceptance, and love?

Imagine yourself holding their suffering within the warmth of your heart. Imagine your heart as a soft warm hug around their suffering.

Know that your heart can hold, nurture, and heal their suffering with love and acceptance.

Understanding the suffering of another

You can begin with a breathing and centering exercise. Come back home to self and ground in your heart space. Remember that you are love. Allow a loved one to come into your awareness.

Ask your loved one if you truly understand their suffering.

Ask them if you have been present for them in their suffering.

Ask them if you were able to hold their suffering without trying to solve or fix.

Look into the suffering of the other person.

Do you really understand what makes them suffer?

Do you accept them even in their suffering?

Do you help them to suffer less by understanding the true sources of their suffering and trying not to add to them?

Imagine yourself embracing them and their suffering. Hold them in a warm hug of love and acceptance. Soften to all of their hard edges. Rest in your own internal love and stability and trust that you will not be shaken by their suffering.

See them in their entirety; struggles, hurts, darkness, beauty, and strength.

Love them in their entirety.

Repeat the following: I love you in all that you are. I love all of you. I love you even when you suffer. I love and accept all of you.

The second quality of Thich Nhat Hanh's true love is happiness. Happiness is the deep seated feeling of peace and acceptance brought on when you know that you are living your heart's truth. In order to find it, we must understand who we truly are and live authentically. In love, we have a desire to find true happiness for ourselves as well as for our loved ones. We understand that our own happiness is not separate from that of our loved ones. If we are looking out for our happiness, we are also looking out for theirs. In wanting them to be happy, we are at the same time wanting ourselves to be happy. If one of us is not living as our authentic self, is not being true to our heart, then neither of us will be genuinely happy in love.

If you want to have true love, then you have to start by being real with yourself, living your own heart's truth, finding your own happiness. You have to stop acting in ways that protect your ego or appeal to other people's expectations. You have to act based on what you are truly feeling and what is really happening inside your heart. You have to tune everything else out and listen only to your heart; then act true to it without fear of how others will respond. If you live true to yourself, then no response can be negative because it is the result of truth. When we are not living in our authenticity, we cannot love because we are not connecting from the heart. Only when we understand and live our own truth, can we feel true happiness and true love.

Once we find our own happiness, it can be very difficult not to have ideas and notions about what would make someone else happy. We often project our own vision of happiness onto our partner in the form of expectations. As Tringpa Rinpoche says, "You should never have expectations for others. Just be kind to them. Setting goals for others can be aggressive- really wanting a success story for ourselves. When we do this to others, we are asking them to live up to our ideals. Instead we should just be kind."[38] We do not know what would make the other person happy. Only they can find and live their true authentic self. So the best we can do is be present for them in open acceptance trying to understand their sources of happiness.

I once heard an explanation of love as learning your loved one's heart song and then gently singing it back to them when they have forgotten. This is what happiness in love means. It means truly understanding the other's heart and guiding them back to it when they have forgotten the way. It is not trying to lead them towards our heart's truth or to our own idea of what their happiness should look like. It's understanding their own happiness so well that we can help them stay true to it.

This requires much courage. It means that we are letting go of control. Instead of holding ownership of our loved one's happiness, we are encouraging them to find it on their own. This also means that we do not depend on our loved one to generate our happiness. We are committed to finding our own heart's truth and authenticity so that we find happiness for ourselves. They are a partner on our journey towards happiness, but they are not the source. We are a partner on their journey, sometimes guiding and redirecting them towards their happiness but never taking ownership of it. In this way, each person is responsible for their own happiness and the loved one is simply there to encourage them to pursue it.

This is very difficult for me. I know what keeps me centered, happy, and healthy, and when my loved ones are struggling I want to convince them to live like me so that they can be happy. It makes it even more difficult having a career as a coach, teaching people how to live mindfully to experience more happiness. I always have to focus on listening more than telling. I use mindfulness as a means to gain a deeper understanding of each person's individual nature and discover what it is that truly makes them happy. I ask a lot of questions and guide them back to their own heart rather than projecting my heart's truth onto them. Sometimes it leads to very different places than I would go in my own life, but I have to let go of control and let their heart guide the way back to their truth.

4.12.3 EXERCISES ON HAPPINESS

Understanding my sources of happiness

You can begin with a breathing and centering exercise. Come back to your center. Reconnect with your heart space and open to listening with the knowledge that the heart space holds our deepest truth.

Ask your heart if you really understand true happiness.

Ask it if you really know what makes you happy.

Are you living as your authentic self?

Are you being true to your heart?

Ask your heart if it feels heard and honored.

Ask your heart if you are living true to it.

In what ways do you turn away from your heart's truth?

Why?

Is it to please others? To meet expectations? To keep your ego or pride safe?

In what ways do you not live as your authentic self?

Is it worth it?

Does it make you truly happy, in a sustainable deep way?

Imagine yourself turning towards the heart, centering in the heart's truth and living authentically.

What does that look like?

Who are you being?

What are you doing?

Is this who you want to be?

Look around you and identify all the true sources of happiness in your life, the ones that reflect your deeper truth. Imagine yourself engaging with these sources of happiness and notice how they return you to your authentic self.

Understanding our loved one's happiness

You can begin with a breathing and centering exercise. Come back to your heart space. Remember that you are love. Bring your loved one into your awareness and hold them in your heart space.

Tell them that you are here for them.

Tell them that you want to understand what truly makes them happy.

Imagine your own heart space opening up and connecting with their heart space. The two inner cores of your being uniting under love, compassion, and acceptance.

Look into their heart and ask them if you really understand their true happiness. Listen for their heart's truth.

Understand that their happiness will lead to your happiness.

Open to seeing their most authentic self. Ask them what truly makes them happy. Learn their heart's song so that you can sing it back to them when they have forgotten.

Tell them that you want them to be happy. That you love them and want them to live their heart's truth.

Notice how they respond and the quality of the energy being shared between your two hearts.

Know that you are both held within that greater energy of love, compassion, and acceptance.

The third quality of Thich Nhat Hanh's true love is Joy. Joy is the playful side of love. It is the laughter, the exploration, and the adventure. We cannot have love without joy. Love can be difficult and it brings with it many challenges, which is why it is so important to cultivate the lighter side of love. Without joy, our love becomes burdensome and stale.

The same is true for loving self. In order to love ourselves fully, we have to connect with our sources of joy. A true practitioner can find joy at any time. All we have to do is become aware of the wonders of life within and around us. We take our focus off the doing, achieving, progressing, and performing and we connect with the beauty of life. We see the miracle of life in all things. This joy of life can be attained at any moment. As you are washing the dishes, look into the miracle of running water. We did not always have fresh water that ran through pipes into our kitchen sink. As you are walking into work, look at the clouds and connect with the wonder of these water molecules that evaporate and condense perfectly to form these beautiful soft wisps in the air. As you breathe, recognize the miracle of breath. This simple action the body performs without much effort to keep us alive and connected to the world around us. These simple things can bring us joy with the right awareness.

We can also connect with joy when we remember the child within. We were not always so disconnected from the simple pleasures. We once found a worm wiggling between our fingers to be a hilarious miracle. We once thought of waves crashing on our toes as a wild adventure. We once saw the forest as a magical playground with endless mysteries to explore. We once saw our friends as playmates to run through the grass with, soaring like birds and bounding like deer. We can reconnect with these simple pleasures at any time by seeing the world once again as a child does, with open hearted wonder.

This joy can show up in our relationship any time that we recognize how lucky we are to have our loved one in our life. When we really see them and acknowledge their presence, we can look our loved one in the eyes and take them all in as we say, "My dear I see that you are here with me and I am so grateful." This is the beginning of joy—simply to recognize the miracle of having this person in our life. When we recognize that they do not have to be there and may not always be there we do not take their presence for granted. Gratitude is the fertilizer for joy.

When we are together, we can reconnect with our childlike

wonder. We can marvel at the fact that we found each other and that we have been gifted this time to spend together. We can laugh and play, explore and adventure. We can try new things and learn new skills. This life is our oyster and we will uncover every pearl. Together, we will discover more and more of the wonders of this miraculous life taking nothing for granted.

4.12.4 EXERCISES ON JOY

Connecting with our sources of joy

You can begin with a breathing and centering exercise. Come back to your center and breathe into your heart space. Allow this space of love, compassion, peace, and acceptance to grow. Know that this is where true awareness of life resides. Look through the eyes of the heart at the world around you.

What miracles do you see in your everyday life?

What are you grateful for that sometimes you forget to see?

Connect with the child within you.

How does this child see the trees, the clouds, the flowers, and the birds? How does this child engage with life?

What does this child enjoy doing?

How does this child play?

Can you bring some of that joy into your current life?

How do you play?

How do you laugh?

How do you explore?

How do you adventure?

What miracles do you see every day?

Feel the joy generated from this awareness of the heart begin to spread through your body and mind. Live the joy.

What does it feel like to live joy?

Who are you being when you are filled with joy?

Bringing joy into our love

You can begin with a breathing and centering exercise. Bring your attention back into your heart space. Invite your loved one into this space with you. Held in the safety of love, compassion, peace, and acceptance, begin to explore your relationship with your loved one.

When you are in their presence, are you aware of how special they are?

Are you aware of their miraculous presence?

Are you grateful to have them in your life?

Do you recognize that they may not always be there?

Look into their eyes and tell them how grateful you are that they are there. Now take their hand and begin to show them all the sources of joy around you. Dance through the open fields. Soar like the birds. Watch the wisps of clouds form and disappear. Wander through the mysteries of the forest.

Look into how you laugh with your loved one.

How you play with your loved one.

How you explore with your loved one.

And how you adventure with your loved one.

Do you try new things?

Do you learn new skills?

Do you look into the wonders of life?

Be together in this joy generated from the awareness of the heart.

How does it feel to be in this joy together?

How do you connect within this joy?

What does your relationship look like within this joy?

The last quality of true love is one of the most difficult for relationships held within the boxes of our society. This quality is freedom. How can we offer freedom in love when we lock it into a contract that binds us to certain expectations and roles? Love cannot be bound within a contract or agreement. It cannot be held to certain rules and laws. It cannot be defined by worldly terms. It is limitless and free. It belongs to no one and yet fills us all. We are love. Paulo Coelho put it beautifully when he said, "Love, I am the beginning of everything and before I existed there was chaos. For me love fills everything. It cannot be desired because it is an end in itself. It cannot be held prisoner because it is a river and will overflow its banks. It cannot betray because it has nothing to do with possession. Anyone who tries to imprison love will cut off the spring that feeds it and the trapped water will go stagnant and rank."[12]

Osho restates the same concept, saying, "Love knows no boundaries. Love cannot be jealous, because love cannot possess. It is ugly, the very idea that you possess somebody because you love. You possess somebody – it means you have killed somebody and turned him into a commodity. Only things can be possessed. Love gives freedom. Love is freedom."[23] So what are these great poets and teachers saying? They are saying that we cannot lock someone into our concepts, ideas, and expectations of what love is and how long it should last. We have to give love and the individuals involved in love the freedom to continuously evolve, transform, and redefine themselves. There is no one form of love. There is no one form of relationship. There is only the energetic feeling of connectedness and oneness that touches us all in different strengths and depths in a wide array of situations and interactions, reminding us that we are not alone on this journey of life.

The first way to give our love freedom is to let go of the notion that our love has to remain the same throughout a lifetime. We will not always love someone in the same way. Our love will evolve and adapt to changes in our awareness and in our being. The yogic way of explaining love relationships is very helpful. They clearly expose the changing nature of love throughout the life of a Grihasta, or lay person. These are the people who choose to marry and live in society. They begin with a love that is more centered on self. This is the Brahmacharya stage, when they are exploring, learning, and gaining wisdom, skills, and knowledge. They then move into the Griha stage, when their love is focused on one individual and family. They find a spouse, enjoy sexual pleasures, and lead a householder's life. They then move into the Vanprastha stage, during which they begin to quiet sexual desires and their love widens beyond the one partner and becomes more centered on gods and spiritual practice. And the final stage is Sonyasa, when they live only a spiritual life much like that of a monk. Here we can clearly see the evolution of love. The spouse does not become insulted when their partner's love is no longer concentrated on them. They allow the love to evolve beyond the marital confines and grow into a more spiritual love for all. There is no hate or resentment when the marital love fades, only acknowledgement of the evolution. There is also no resentment or hatred when in the younger stages love is more self-oriented and individuals are not focused on loving one person but on finding their own wisdom, knowledge, and skills. No one is insulted that they are focused on self. It is simply seen as a certain step on love's transformative journey. They are still loving, it just looks different. The marital love concentrated on one individual and family only occupies a short period in life. There is no expectation that it will remain unchanging forever.

It is never love that hurts us but the expectations and demands that we build on the notion of love. If we are able to love without contaminating it with our own notions of what it should be and what it should offer us, then we would never suffer in love. Without our notions, we can live in peace with what is. When we give love freedom, we prioritize love over relationship. We love love more than we love relationship. The relationship may end, but love will remain.

Love and the individuals in it will evolve because both are free. Only possession stays rigid and unchanging. We possess because we are afraid of change. As Thich Nhat Hanh says, "We do not suffer because things are impermanent but because we believe that things are permanent and when they change, we feel deceived and hurt."[19] If we see that all things are impermanent, then we can love the other fully in this moment without expecting them to always stay the same. We know that this person continues to evolve and change in each moment and will never be the same from one moment to the next. We give them the freedom to continue to change and evolve without the fear of losing them. As Morrie in the book *Tuesdays with Morrie* states, "When you love someone, you care more about their situation than your own."[2] We love the other person so much that we prefer their happiness over our need for them to play a certain role in our life or meet certain expectations associated with our relational contract. We understand that their happiness is our happiness, and we encourage them to change and evolve on their journey towards their own truth.

In this freedom, we know that our loved one does not constantly have to be by our side living as we live. We allow them the space necessary to pursue their own interests, learning, and growth. When we see a beautiful flower from a distance surrounded by a whole meadow of complementary colors and textures, we love it for what it is. If we want the flower to belong to us simply because we love it, and we pick it from the meadow, grasping it in our hands, we cut it off from the life force that made it beautiful. Slowly but surely, it will begin to die, and although we will be in possession of it, it will no longer be the same beautiful flower we loved. Our loved one has to continue to live as an individual while still relating to us. If we try to capture our loved one and hold them too close, they will lose their unique beauty. We do not own our loved one simply because we love them. We love them because of who they are, and in order to remain who they are, they have to be given the freedom to continue down their own unique path.

This amount of freedom requires a deep trust of self, of love, and of the greater system. If we don't trust, then we feel the need to control our partner by locking them into a specific role that we and society have defined for them. This gives us the false security that nothing will ever change, and that they will always be there for us in exactly the way we expect them to. Trust means that we let go of the need to control the outcome. We don't need a guarantee for the future. We trust that we will be okay no matter what happens because we have developed all of the tools necessary to live our own truth and happiness. We trust that love will remain, no matter what happens to our relationship, knowing that love is so much bigger than its one role in this one connection. We trust the greater system to know better than we do what belongs on our journey. We let go of our own notion of the good outcome and trust that what happens is exactly what is meant to happen. All these levels of trust allow us to give our love and our loved one the freedom to grow, evolve, and thrive.

I always think about my mom when contemplating the freedom of love. I brought her much joy when I was young and living at home. I fit one role within the family that met many of her needs for companionship, support, love, and a listening ear. Then when I was sixteen, I left for a one year exchange program in Switzerland. To me, she showed endless support, but once I was gone, she went home and cried and cried. It was very hard for her to give me freedom because her happiness was dependent on me playing one role in her life. But after that moment, we developed a new kind of relationship—one where she gave me all the freedom in the world to move, explore, grow, and fail. She was supportive of any idea I had, and loved me through all of the big changes in my life. It ended up deepening her love and understanding of me because she got to experience the real me free of her own concept of who I should be or what role I should play. She got to know me in all of the different places I lived, jobs I had, roles I played, relationships I engaged in, and failures I faced. It helped her to grow in her own life through all of the experiences she had while engaging in mine. At first, the choice that led to her losing me ended up helping us to find each other on a whole new level.

4.12.5 EXERCISES ON GRANTING LOVE FREEDOM

Freeing love

You can begin with a breathing and centering exercise. Come back home to self and reconnect with your mind, body, and spirit. Open to observing self without judgment. We are not trying to fix, solve, or condemn. We are simply observing so that we can understand self better. With this open-minded acceptance, begin to explore your notions of love.

What do you think love is?

What do you think it should feel like?

What do you think it should do for you?

What are your expectations of love?

Now examine your love for someone in your life.

What expectations do you put on that love?

What role do you believe they should play in your life simply because you love them?

What contracts have you assigned to your love?

How much freedom have you given that love to evolve and change?

Can you feel the difference between love and possession?

Between love and need?

Between love and dependence?

Between love and relationship?

Release your grasp on your love for this person. Step back from it and allow it to drift out in front of you. Release your need to control it and own it. Allow it to move freely within and around you. Release your need to define it into certain roles and categories. Allow it to take on any form it wants.

Release your need for this love to remain the same. Allow it to morph, change, and evolve in any way it wants. Watch as you give it this freedom and feel its true nature.

Does it belong to you?

Is it rigid and unchanging?

What does it feel like to give love freedom?

Feel the peace and ease it gives you to trust love. To know that it will always be present. Know that it will remain even if you let go of your controlling grasp on it.

Trust that love is in you and around you. Trust that love is always present because you are love.

Loving freely

You can begin with a breathing and centering exercise. Follow the breath back into your heart space. Feel this space filled with nothing but love, compassion, peace, and acceptance, and gratitude. Know that the heart is nothing but love and that love is the center of your being. Holding onto this love, bring a loved one into your awareness.

Look at them from a distance as though you were not present in their life. Watch how they interact with the world. Watch how they interact with self. Watch how they play, learn, and grow. Watch what makes them happy. Watch what makes them suffer. As you watch them, look into what you love about them.

What makes them uniquely them?

What about their uniqueness do you love?

Now come into interaction with them. Allow your love to be present without trying to possess them. Love without needing. Love without demanding. Love without expectations.

Imagine loving them while allowing them complete freedom to remain who they are.

Imagine loving them while offering them the space to continue to walk their own path.

Notice how you can continue to relate to one another even in this freedom and space. Notice how you love who they are as an individual and who they are in relation to you. Understand that you can walk with each other without controlling their every step.

In freedom, you can still find each other and love each other.

It is not possible to experience and maintain true love without boundaries. Boundaries are needed in order for us to fully express compassion, to feel happiness and joy, and to give freedom. They are our way of holding responsibility for our own well-being. They are the foundation of our trust in self. They allow us to take ownership of how we respond to other's behavior, knowing that it is our responsibility to tell them what is okay and what is not instead of simply judging them for what they do and then feeling hurt and angry.

Boundaries help us to be compassionate; they help us to take care of our own well-being so that we can show up in a healthy way for others. In her research on compassion, Brene Brown discovered that the one thing all of the world's most compassionate people had in common was well-defined boundaries. She says that "Compassionate people ask for what they need. They say no when they need to, and when they say yes, they mean it. They're compassionate because their boundaries keep them out of resentment."[9] We can be kind to others only when we are kind to ourselves and being kind to ourselves means that we ask for what we need and how we want to be treated. If we allow ourselves to be walked all over and taken advantage of, then our anger and resentment prevent us from showing up with integrity for others. Compassion is strongest when we are seated within our own strength and integrity. We then can be present for others as our whole and balanced self.

Without boundaries, it will be difficult to feel happiness. True happiness is experienced when we are living as our true authentic self. If we don't have well-established boundaries, we most likely are living based on other people's needs and expectations instead of our own, and this will prevent us from living authentically. When we aren't living our own happiness, it becomes very difficult to nurture and support the happiness of our loved ones. We begin to expect them to meet our needs and expectations just like we have been breaking our backs to meet theirs. This leads to no one being happy.

Joy is felt when we are living one hundred percent in the present fully aware of the miracles within and around us. If we have not established healthy boundaries, we may be feeling taken advantage of or hurt, and this makes it very difficult to live in the present. We get stuck on resentments of the past or fears of what may happen in the future. Boundaries allow us to live in the present because they assure us that we have lived true to ourselves in the past and that we will be capable of taking care of ourselves in the future. We know that we have set ourselves up for success in our relationships and don't need to live in worry. This frees us up to engage in the joy of the present.

The trust required to allow freedom within our love and relationships is built on the integrity of our boundaries. Healthy boundaries give us the guarantee that no matter what other people do, we will keep ourselves healthy and well. They set up a plan of action so that when hurtful behavior arises in our relationship, we both know exactly what to do to keep ourselves safe. Boundaries are not expectations or ultimatums; they are "if, then" statements that help us stay true to our well-being when someone's behavior is no longer supporting our growth and integrity. With this safety procedure set in place, we can give our loved ones freedom to follow their own truth while knowing that we have the tools necessary to take care of our own well-being through all of the changes.

Establishing a boundary requires a very deep awareness of our own truth and what we need in order to maintain our well-being. We have to know where our limitations are and at what point we lose the ability to care for ourselves. A boundary needs to be set before we hit these limits. This awareness comes from all the previous work we have done on this mindful journey. We get in touch with what we are experiencing when a loved one does or says certain things and understand why it affects us the way it does. This allows us to establish a clear and focused boundary that helps our loved one to understand exactly why certain behaviors are hurtful to us. We have to communicate in a way that is loving and peaceful so that they can hear us as we share our truth. We have to be strong enough to maintain the boundary and then we have to be open enough to continually reexamine the boundaries we have set to make sure they are still effective. A boundary is not an order or a command. It is an "if, then" statement that lets your loved one know your truth about how certain behaviors make you feel and how you will take care of yourself if they arise.

For example:

When I have to do all the household chores alone, I become overwhelmed and feel taken advantage of, which leads to resentment. If you cannot help me with them, then I will have to budget in a housekeeper to relieve some of the burden.

When we spend so much time together, I start having deeper feelings for you, and then you push me away. It's very hurtful because I feel rejected and unloved. If you cannot be open to having a relationship with me, I will need to take some distance from you so that I don't develop unrequited feelings.

When you bring up politics, it always leads to a fight and it makes me feel disrespected and unheard. If you cannot be around me without bringing up politics, then I will need to distance myself from you until you can so that we no longer get into arguments that are hurtful to both of us.

All of these boundaries clearly explain the truth of your experience through vulnerability and then give an option to the other person. Either they can reexamine their behavior and alter it so that you can remain safe, or you will take the appropriate action to take care of your own well-being. They are not a demand on the other person, simply a request with an option to alter their behavior or accept a change in ours. They are meant to keep both parties safe and healthy and living true to themselves.

4.12.6 EXERCISES ON ESTABLISHING BOUNDARIES

Understanding your limits

You may want to begin by returning to the section on finding your own truth so that you can be fully honest with your own experience. Start with a breathing and centering exercise. Come back to your heart and listen to your truth.

What in your relationship is making it hard for you to take care of your own well-being?

Where and how are you compromising your own truth?

You may be able to identify these things by working backwards from a point where you were pushed past your limit and behaved in a harmful way to self or to your loved one. Notice how you were feeling in that moment.

What needs weren't being met?

What emotions were you feeling?

What parts of your truth weren't you living?

Now rewind from the hurtful moment and notice when the feelings started to build. Notice those first steps you took away from your own truth. Recognize when you may have said yes to something you didn't really want to do, or when you went quiet and accepted when you had something different to say. Notice when you tried to meet someone else's needs or expectations even when it meant not being true to yourself. This is the limit that you need to set a boundary at: before you hit your hurtful state.

Notice what taking care of yourself before reaching your limit would have looked like.

What would you have done to step away from the edge?

How could you have nurtured yourself before feeling hurt and angry at the other person?

Imagine setting a boundary there.

What would it look like?

What would you say?

How would you take care of yourself?

What does it feel like to be living within the safety of this healthy boundary?

Notice how healthy boundaries allow you to feel safe with this other person. They build a trust of self that you can honor your own truth and your own heart and they build a trust of the other person to listen and honor your needs. Notice how the trust built from healthy boundaries actually allows you to connect deeper and love fuller.

Sharing your boundary with your loved one

After completing the previous exercise, you can put it into words for your loved one. Share your own truth and vulnerability so that they understand why you need this boundary. Explain how accepting their behavior is hurtful to your well-being. Let them know what you will do to take care of yourself if they cannot alter their behavior. You can use the following guide if it helps.

Guide: When _____(explain the hurtful behavior) I feel _____(explain what needs aren't being met or what vulnerabilities are being triggered) which leads to _____(explain the unhealthy reactions it brings up in you) _____If you cannot _____(the desired change in behavior from them) then I will _____(how you will change your behavior to take care of your own well-being.)

Our true nature is love. We all have the capacity to love and to accept love. The only thing holding us back are the barriers we build around ourselves from fear, misunderstanding, and pride. Once we let go of these self-protective mechanisms and open to our true loving nature, our relationships flourish. Love is never harmful, it never disappoints, it never betrays, and it never disappears. It is the constant energy of life that runs within us, around us, and through us. We cannot lose love because we are love.

13

Living From the Heart

Hope is what keeps us moving forward on the path towards transformation of self and the world. Without hope for the possibility of healing, there is no reason to continue. As soon as we stop believing that change is possible, we become stuck; we stop trying to look for all the possibilities for growth and evolution. As soon as we stop believing that healing is possible, we stop engaging with all of the positive sources of change in the world. With a simple glimmer of hope, our eyes and hearts are open to every door, window, and crack that may lead to the source of healing.

Desire is not the same thing as hope. Desire is filled with clinging and grasping, and usually involves the prescription of one possible "good" outcome. Desire leaves us feeling let down and deceived when this one good outcome does not manifest. It can trap us in despair because things aren't turning out the way we envisioned. It can leave us blind to all of the miraculous occurrences happening at every moment because all we have eyes for is the one thing we had our mind set on.

Hope, on the other hand, is the ability to find the good in everything that we encounter. It is our ability to find meaning in every experience. After surviving the death camps of the Holocaust, Victor Frankl found that what was needed to keep people alive in the most dire of situations is meaning. He said that "those who survive are those oriented toward the future, toward meaning to be fulfilled by them in the future."[16] Hope for the future is what allows us to find meaning in any experience. Instead of only seeing the good in the outcome that we desire, we see the good in every situation because we know that we can use it for self-transcendence.

In order to feel hope we need a clear vision of what it is we believe in. This belief keeps us on our own spiritual path because we trust that our work is moving towards a more positive world. Anne Frank explains what keeps her living with virtue, saying "It's really a wonder that I haven't dropped all my ideals, because they seem so absurd and impossible to carry out. Yet I keep them, because in spite of everything, I still believe that people are really good at heart."[15] She maintains her ideals because she trusts that people really are good and that there is hope for positive transformation.

Living with hope is living with intention. It means that we hold onto a vision of what humans are capable of when aligned with the heart's true essence and we live with the intention to arrive at that vision. It's a process of letting go of our own desires and wants in order to serve the vision of the greater human possibility. We devote ourselves to the healing of all beings. We trust that when we live every day serving this hope and intention, that our every experience will be exactly what we need to move forward on the path towards healing.

To engage with these intentions, we reconnect with our own heart. We remember that at our center, there is nothing but love, peace, compassion, acceptance, and gratitude. We remember what the heart values most and what it prioritizes. We remember who we really want to be and how we want to show up for ourselves, others, and our planet. Then we can expand that heart space beyond self. We recognize that the whole world has this same core, and that love runs through everything. Under all the layers of hurt, pain, and trauma, love is still the strongest force. And we allow this knowing to create our hopeful intentions motivating us to continue practicing so that we can heal ourselves and in turn heal the world.

You can use the following exercise to connect with your inner hope.

4.13.1 EXERCISE ON CONNECTING WITH YOUR INNER HOPE

Connecting with hope

You can begin with a breathing and centering exercise. Bring your attention into your heart space. Remember the values of the heart: love, peace, compassion, acceptance, and gratitude. Remember what the heart values most and what it prioritizes. Reconnect with who you really want to be out in the world and how you want to show up for self, others, and the world.

What do you want to offer the world?

What do you want to receive from it?

Allow each breath to expand and open your heart wider and wider. Imagine the heart expanding past all your layers of doubt, worry, the can'ts and impossibilities.

The larger the heart gets, the stronger hope becomes.

Allow the hope to take over the whole heart space and expand outwards into the world. Feel the hope moving out of your own being and connecting with the spirit of all of life. Feel as your own desires and wants drop away and the greater human possibility takes over your entire being.

Trust the vision of this potential. From this place of trust, allow hope to run wild. Allow it to take over your mind and create a vision for the future. Quiet any form of doubt or denial. Hand yourself over to hope.

Observe the beautiful vision it creates. Play in its creativity. Allow the vision to expand as large as it wants. Now feel what it's like to live in this vision.

How do you feel?

What are you seeing, hearing, smelling, and feeling?

What is the nature of all beings?

How are you interacting?

What are we prioritizing?

Who are you being in this world?

Allow yourself to believe in the possibility and set intentions for giving yourself over to the cultivation of this greater human potential. Offer yourself to the healing of all beings and trust that you can do it.

Hold these intentions in your heart and your core and allow them to integrate into every fiber of your being.

This is your heart's true essence.

With hope, we continue with the practice, knowing that with each day that we choose to cultivate more light, love, peace, kindness, compassion, acceptance, and gratitude, we heal ourselves and the world.

This hope keeps us motivated to continue practicing, because we know that healing the mind, body, and spirit is a never ending process. We are constantly coming in and out of balance. Old habits pop back up. Our past traumas get triggered. Past pains rise to the surface. It is our mindful practice that keeps us aware of these fluctuations in our balance and brings us back to our center, the heart. The heart is our core essence, who we really are when we are in balance. It is nothing but **LOVE, PEACE, COMPASSION, ACCEPTANCE,** and **GRATITUDE.**

The energies of the heart are so much bigger than just us. They are interconnected to all other life forms in the universe. Their energy is the life force that runs through us all. They are always accessible if we just remember to tune in. They are more powerful than any other force and are capable of healing all suffering. When you are living from the heart, you are tapped into this life force and become capable of anything. In connecting with the heart, you connect with your authentic self, your true nature. You remember what you are here to do and trust that you are on the right path.

Every action motivated by the heart creates healing and growth in you and in the world around you. The steps of your life start to align naturally, and although they may be challenging, there is a lightness to your path brought on by hope and inspiration. You are no longer fighting upstream to get to where you believe you should end up. The river of life flows freely beneath you, carrying you on your purposeful journey. You may not know exactly where you are headed, but you know this is where you are meant to be.

4.13.2 LIVING FROM THE HEART

Joining the flow of life

You can begin with a breathing and centering exercise. Bring your attention into your heart space. Remember the values of the heart: love, peace, compassion, acceptance, and gratitude. Remember what the heart values most and what it prioritizes. Reconnect with who you really want to be out in the world and how you want to show up for self, others, and the world.

Feel the energies of the heart. Notice how they expand beyond you. How they flow within you and out into the world around you connecting all things.

Feel how powerful these forces are. See their light energy. Recognize that they are capable of healing all suffering. Explore their potential. Notice that they are limitless.

Allow their limitless potential to build a trust within you. Trust that if you are living with these forces within and around you, that you, too, are capable of all things. Give yourself over to the energies of the heart. Allow them to carry you as you give up your own struggle.

Let go of your need to push and fight the world. Let go of your need to control all outcomes and the destination of your path. Give yourself over to the energies of the heart and trust that they will carry you where you need to go.

Lean back on the river of life—the river created by the energies of the heart. Allow them to flow within and around you. Give yourself over to the flow. Feel its power beneath you. Feel it guiding you to your true purpose. Feel it lifting you up to your full potential.

Become the energies of the heart.

Live from the energies of the heart.

Acknowledgments

There are so many amazing teachers who have inspired the lessons in this book. Whether I've met them in person, read their books, listened to their podcasts and Dharma talks, or met them in everyday life, they all contributed to my own healing insights. I would say my greatest teacher and healer is Mother Nature. She has been there for me ever since I was a child. In her forests and mountains I find my inner strength, peace, acceptance, and courage. Some of my most challenging moments have happened in her presence and they have taught me what I need to carry within in order to survive. She continues to be a place of serenity for me where I return over and over to receive wisdom.

My second greatest teacher is Thich Nhat Hanh. I only met him once, but through his practices, books, Dharma talks, and essence, I fell in love with mindfulness. He lives the practice so thoroughly that you can't help but absorb it in his presence. He makes mindfulness simple and accessible to everyone taking out the barriers of complication set up by many Buddhist teachings. If you truly live his practice, you will experience peace and happiness in your life.

I would also like to thank my mom. She has always been my

biggest fan and cheerleader. Her desire to be a part of my life brought her from translating the Bible in Kenya to Thich Nhat Hanh's monastery in France where our healing began. She was one of my first clients and witnessing her transformation inspired me to continue my work. Her faith in me gives me the courage and strength to continue forward on this mindful journey even when it seems like we're the only ones who truly understand its healing powers.

About the Author

Erin Easton is a mindfulness based life coach in Montrose, Colorado. After eleven years of teaching French, Spanish and English, Erin decided to teach something more meaningful, a way to find true happiness. She leads group mindfulness sessions and offers individual coaching for people who want to balance their mind, body, and spirit reawakening their heart's wisdom. She also leads wilderness retreats on which clients use Mother Nature to assist in growing self-awareness and collective insight.

The first time Erin began to connect with mindfulness was when she was recovering from a three year back injury and sought healing in a meditation class at the Shedrob Choekhor Ling monastery outside of Geneva Switzerland. After a year of meditation and philosophy classes at the monastery, she participated in a retreat at Thich Nhat Hanh's monastery, Plum Village, in France. This is where she fell in love with mindfulness. She continued to practice with a sangha in Geneva and changed the focus of her master's degree in French to the effects of mindfulness and meditation on language acquisition. She studied the use of mindfulness in schools with Educ-Inspir, a French branch of Wakeup Schools created by Thich Nhat Hanh. She participated in a Vipassana retreat and did a three month study internship at Tara Mandala Buddhist Center outside of Pagosa Springs Colorado, but finds her true mindful roots in the Plum Village Tradition of Thich Nhat Hanh.

Erin began her career as a mindfulness instructor in schools using the practice in her language classes and offering elective classes in Brain Science and Mindfulness. Soon, she discovered that mindfulness was all she wanted to teach and she left the school environment to start her own coaching business. Erin grew up in a Christian family but never found her spiritual home there. After years of exploring different religions and practices she was able to find that true heart wisdom can be found anywhere. She uses mindful awareness to connect individuals with their own wisdom so that they too can build a spirituality that speaks their heart's truth.

Erin's goal in life is to end the suffering of as many individuals as possible by reconnecting them to the wisdom within and around them. She helps people to listen to the truth within their own heart so they can start living as their authentic self with more peace, purpose, and happiness.

www.newleafmindfulness.com
erinkeaston@gmail.com

Resources

Section 1

1. Doidge, N. (2007). The Brain That Changes Itself: Stories of Personal Triumph from the Frontiers of Brain Science. United States: Penguin Publishing Group.
2. Hawkins, D.R (2013) Reality, Spirituality, and Modern Man. Hay House Inc., U.S.
3. Immordino-Yang, M. n.d. 2011 "Me, My '"self"' and You: Neuropsycho- Logical Relations between Social Emotion, Self-Awareness, and Morality." *Emotion Review* 3: 313–15.
4. Martucci, Fadel, et al, Katherine, Zeidan. 2014. "Neural Correlates of Mindfulness Meditation-Related Anxiety Relief." *2Department of Biomedical Engineering, Wake Forest School of Medicine, Medical Center Boulevard* 9: 751–59.

Section 2

1. Achor Shaw, (2011) The Happiness Advantage, retrieved from https://www.youtube.com/watch?v=GXy__kBVq1M
2. Adolphb, Rohdea, et al, Drik, Katharina. 2014. "Mindful Attention Regulation and Non-Judgmental Orientation

in Depression: A Multi-Method Approach." *Biological Psychology* 101 (July): 36–43.
3. Anderson, Farb, Adam, Norman. 2010. "Minding One's Emotions: Mindfulness Training Alters the Neural Expression of Sadness." *American Psychological Association* 10 (1): 25–33.
4. Bhattacharjee, Y. (2020) A World of Pain, National Geographic, Jan 2020
5. Brach, Tara. (2014, Apr 17) RAIN: Cultivating a Mindful Awareness. Retrieved from https://www.youtube.com/watch?v=HdviZ2lSxfc&t=86s
6. Bradberry, T., Greaves, J. (2009). Emotional Intelligence 2.0. United States: TalentSmart.
7. Brainard, G., Greeson, J., Reibel, D., Rosenzweig, S., (2001) Mindfulness-based stress reduction and health-related quality of life in a heterogeneous patient population, General Hospital Psychiatry 23 (2001) 183–192
8. Brown, K.W., (2003) The benefits of being present: mindfulness and its role in psychological well-being. KW Brown, RM Ryan - Journal of personality and social psychology, 84:4, 822
9. Chopra, D. (2014). The Future of God: A Practical Approach to Spirituality for Our Times. United States: Potter/Ten Speed/Harmony/Rodale.
10. Cushieri, David, quoted in goodreads.com/quotes.
11. Delongis, A., Folkman, S., Lazarus, R. (1988) The Impact of Daily Stress on Health and Mood: Psychological and Social Resources as Mediators, Journal of Personality and Social Psychology, Vol. 54. No. 3.486-495

12. Doidge, N. (2007). The Brain That Changes Itself: Stories of Personal Triumph from the Frontiers of Brain Science. United States: Penguin Publishing Group.
13. Duncan, Dowsett, et al., G.J., C. J. 2007. "School Readiness and Later Achievement." *Developmental Psychology*, 43: 1428–46.
14. Eckman, Davidson, RicardWallace, P, R.J., M., A. 2005. "Buddhist and Psychological Perspectives on Emotion and Well-Being." *Current Directions in Psychological Science* 14 (2): 59–63.
15. Einstein, Albert quoted in goodreads.com/quotes
16. Farb, Garland, Huston, Norman, Eric, Daniel. 2011. "Mechanisms of Mindfulness in Communication Training." *Journal of Applied Communication Research* 39 (4)
17. Fichera, E., Ohrnberger, J., Sutton, M., (2017) The relationship between physical and mental health: A mediation analysis, Social Science & Medicine, Volume 195, 42-49
18. Flooke, Goldberg, et al, Lisa, Simon B. 2013. "Mindfulness for Teachers: A Pilot Study to Assess Effects on Stress, Burnout, and Teaching Efficacy." *International Mind, Brain, and Education Society and Blackwell Publishing, Inc.* 7 (3).
19. Frankl, V. E. (2011). The Unheard Cry for Meaning: Psychotherapy and Humanism. United States: Touchstone.
20. Gatto, J. T. (2010). Weapons of Mass Instruction: A Schoolteacher's Journey Through the Dark World of Compulsory Schooling. United States: New Society Publishers.
21. Goleman, David (2009) Emotional intelligence: What it is and do men or women have more of it, Big Think, http://bigthink.com/ideas/14673?jwsource=cl

22. Hanh, T. N. (1996). Living Buddha, Living Christ. United Kingdom: Rider.
23. Hawkins, D. R. (2016). The Eye of the I: From Which Nothing Is Hidden. United States: Hay House.
23.) Hawkins, D.R (2013) Reality, Spirituality, and Modern Man. Hay House Inc., U.S.
24. Hennely, Sarah. 2011. "The Immediate and Sustained Effects of the .b Mindfulness Programme on Adolescents' Social and Emotional Well-Being and Academic Functioning." *Oxford Brookes University*, September.
1. Inzlicht, Rimma, Zindel, Michael, Tepper, Segal. 2013. "Inside the Mindful Mind: How Mindfulness Enhances Emotion Regulation Through Improvements in Executive Control." *University of Toronto Current Directions in Psychological Science* 22 (6): 449–54.
2. Jones, Hansen, Susan M., Wesley. 2014. "The Impact of Mindfulness on Supportive Communication Skills: Three Exploratory Studies." *Springer and Science Business Media*, November.
3. Kabat-Zinn, J. (2009). Wherever You Go, There You Are: Mindfulness Meditation In Everyday Life. United States: Hachette Books.
4. Kempson, Joseph Robert. n.d. "Mindfulness in Schools A Mixed Methods Investigation of How Secondary School Pupils Perceive the Impact of Studying Mindfulness in School and the Barriers to Its Successful Implementation." *CARDIFF UNIVERSITy, Doctorate in Educational Psychology*, 2009–12.

5. Kung, Hans cited in Hanh, T. N. (1996). Living Buddha, Living Christ. United Kingdom: Rider.
6. Laozi. (1972). Tao te ching. New York :Vintage Books,
7. Ledoux, J. (2015). The Emotional Brain: The Mysterious Underpinnings of Emotional Life. United States: Simon & Schuster.
8. Markman, Art. (2014) Two Guys on Your Head, Automaticity, KUT.org
9. Martucci, Fadel, et al, Katherine, Zeidan. 2014. "Neural Correlates of Mindfulness Meditation-Related Anxiety Relief." *2Department of Biomedical Engineering, Wake Forest School of Medicine, Medical Center Boulevard* 9: 751–59.
10. Merton, Thomas (1966) as cited in Palmer, P. J. (2009). A Hidden Wholeness: The Journey Toward an Undivided Life. United Kingdom: Wiley.
11. Pagels, E. (2004). The Gnostic Gospels. United States: Random House Publishing Group.
12. Posner, Rothbart, M. L., M. K. n.d. 1998 "Attention, Self-Regulation and Consciousness." *Philosophical Transactions of the Royal Society B: Biological Sciences,* 353 (1377): 1915–27.
13. Rock, David (2010) New Study Shows Humans Are On Autopilot Nearly Half the Time, Your Brain At Work, Psychology Today; Nov 14, 2010. www.psychologytoday.com/us/blog/your-brain-work
14. Semple, Lee, Rosa, Randye, Jennifer, Dinelia. 2010. "A Randomized Trial of Mindfulness-Based Cognitive Therapy for Children: Promoting Mindful Attention to Enhance Social-Emotional Resiliency in Children." *Springer Science+Business Media* 19: 218–29.

15. Snyder, M. (1980). Seek, and ye shall find: Testing hypotheses about other people. In E. T. Higgins, C. P. Herman, & M. P. Zanna (Eds.), Social cognition: The Ontario Symposium on Personality and Social Psychology (Vol. 1, pp. 105–130). Hillsdale, NJ: Lawrence Erlbaum Associates.
16. Taylor, Jill B., (2008) My Stroke of Insight, Ted Talks, https://youtu.be/UyyjU8fzEYU
17. The Gospel of Mary Magdalene as cited in Bourgeault, C. (2010). The Meaning of Mary Magdalene: Discovering the Woman at the Heart of Christianity. United States: Shambhala.
18. The Gospel of Thomas as cited in Pagels, E. (2004). The Gnostic Gospels. United States: Random House Publishing Group.
19. Tolle, E. (2008). A New Earth: Awakening to Your Life's Purpose. United Kingdom: Plume.
20. Wolkin, Jennifer. 2015. "Cultivating Multiple Aspects of Attention through Mindfulness Meditation Accounts for Psychological Well-Being through Decreased Rumination." *Dove Press Journal*, June.

Section 3 and 4

1. Ajahn Brahm. (2019, Nov 18) Building Resilience. Retrieved from https://www.youtube.com/watch?v=_znbRN8JRXw
2. Albom, M. (2007). Tuesdays with Morrie: An Old Man, a Young Man, and Life's Greatest Lesson, 20th Anniversary Edition. United Kingdom: Crown.
3. Ball-Rokeach, S.J., Defleur, M.L. (1976) A Dependency

Model of Mass Media Effects. Communication Research. Vol 3 N. 1, Jan 1976

4. Bandura, A. (2001) Social Cognitive Theory of Mass Communication, Media Psychology, Department of Psychology Stanford University, 3, 265–299.

5. Barry, C., Sidoti, C., Briggs, S., Reiter, S., Lindsey, R., (2017) Adolescent social media use and mental health from adolescent and parent perspectives. Journal of adolescents, 61 (2017) 1-11

6. Bekalu, M. A., McCloud, R. F., & Viswanath, K. (2019). Association of Social Media Use With Social Well-Being, Positive Mental Health, and Self-Rated Health: Disentangling Routine Use From Emotional Connection to Use. *Health Education & Behavior*, 46(2_suppl), 69S-80S.https://doi.org/10.1177/1090198119863768

7. Beutel, Manfred E et al. "Noise Annoyance Is Associated with Depression and Anxiety in the General Population-The Contribution of Aircraft Noise." *PloS one* vol. 11,5 e0155357. 19 May. 2016, doi:10.1371/journal.pone.0155357

8. Brown, B. (2010). The Gifts of Imperfection. United States: Hazelden Publishing.

9. Brown, B. (2017). Braving the Wilderness: The Quest for True Belonging and the Courage to Stand Alone. United States: Random House Publishing Group.

10. Cantor, J. (2008). Fright reactions to mass media. In Jennings Bryant and Mary Beth Oliver (eds.), Media Effects: Advances in Theory and Research, pp. 287-306. Routledge

11. Chödrön, P. (2004). Start where You are: A Guide to Compassionate Living. United States: Shambhala.

12. Coelho, P. (2009). The Witch of Portobello: A Novel. United States: HarperOne
13. Djupesland, Per G et al. "Accessing the brain: the nose may know the way." *Journal of cerebral blood flow and metabolism : official journal of the International Society of Cerebral Blood Flow and Metabolism* vol. 33,5 (2013): 793-4. doi:10.1038/jcbfm.2013.41
14. Emerson, R.W. as cited in Palmer, P. J. (2009). A Hidden Wholeness: The Journey Toward an Undivided Life. United Kingdom: Wiley.
15. Frank, A. (2018). The Diary of a Young Girl. Italy: Vividing Inc..
16. Frankl, V. E. (2011). The Unheard Cry for Meaning: Psychotherapy and Humanism. United States: Touchstone.
17. Granovetter, M. (1983). The strength of weak ties—A network theory revisited. In R. Collins (Ed.), Sociological theory 1983 (pp. 201–233). San Francisco: Jossey-Bass.
18. Hanh, T. N. (2013). The Art of Communicating. United States: HarperOne.
19. Hanh, T. N. (2012). The Pocket Thich Nhat Hanh. United States: Shambhala.
20. Hanh, T.N. (2010). Reconciliation: Healing the Inner Child. Berkley CA, Parallax Press
21. Harris, M. B., & Evans, R. C. (1973). Models and Creativity. Psychological Reports, 33(3), 763–769. https://doi.org/10.2466/pro.1973.33.3.763
22. Hunt, M. G., Marx, R., Lipson, C., and Young, J., (2018). No More FOMO: Limiting Social Media Decreases

Loneliness and Depression. Journal of Social and Clinical Psychology: Vol. 37, No. 10, pp. 751-768.
23. Intimacy: Trusting Oneself and the Other. (2007). United States: St. Martin's Press.
24. I-Safe. (2004) Cyber Bullying Statistics and Tips. https://auth.isafe.org/outreach/media/media_cyber_bullying
25. Kornfield, J. (2009). The Wise Heart: A Guide to the Universal Teachings of Buddhist Psychology. United States: Bantam Books.
26. Kunzig, R. (2020) A World Without Trash. National Geographic. Jan 2020
27. Lemieux, R., Lajoie, S., & Trainor, N. E. (2013). Affinity-seeking, social loneliness, and social avoidance among Facebook users.Psychological Reports: Mental&Physical Health, 112, 545e552.
28. Milgram, S. (1974). Obedience to authority: An experimental view. New York: Harper & Row.
29. Nass, C., (2012). Is Facebook Stunting Your Child's Growth?, The Pacific Standard: April 23
30. Palmer, P. J. (2009). A Hidden Wholeness: The Journey Toward an Undivided Life. United Kingdom: Wiley.
31. Pew Research Center. (2019). Social Media Fact Sheet. https://www.pewresearch.org/internet/fact-sheet/social-media/
32. Pew Research Center. (2015).Teens, social media, and technology overview 2015.http://www.pewinternet.org/2015/04/09/teens-social-media-technology-2015.
33. Rogers, E. M., & Kincaid, D. L. (1981). Communication

networks: Toward a new paradigm for research. New York: Free Press.
34. Rumi quoted in goodreads.com/quotes
35. Schmidt, A.L., Zollo, F., et. al., (2017) Anatomy of News Consumption on Facebook, Proceedings of the National Academy of Sciences Mar 2017, 114 (12) 3035-3039; DOI: 10.1073/pnas.1617052114
36. Subrahmanyam, Smahel, & Greenfield, 2006, Connecting Online Behavior to Adolescent Development: A Theoretical Framework, Digital Youth, Feb 2010, 10.1007/978-1-4419-6278-2_2
37. Tolle, E. (2008). A New Earth: Awakening to Your Life's Purpose. United Kingdom: Plume.
38. Tringpa Rinpoche as cited in Chödrön, P. (2004). Start where You are: A Guide to Compassionate Living. United States: Shambhala.
39. Williams, Florence. "The Nature Fix." W. W. Norton & Company, Inc. 2017
40. Woods, H. C., & Scott, H. (2016). #Sleepyteens: Social media use in adolescence is associated with poor sleep quality, anxiety, depression, and low self-esteem.Journal of Adolescence, 51,41e49.

www.ingramcontent.com/pod-product-compliance
Lightning Source LLC
Chambersburg PA
CBHW071956290426
44109CB00018B/2037